S0-AFU-755

FOURTH and LONG

FOURTH and LONG

The Kent Waldrep Story

KENT WALDREP
and
SUSAN MARY MALONE

CROSSROAD · NEW YORK

1996

The Crossroad Publishing Company
370 Lexington Avenue, New York, NY 10017

Library of Congress Cataloging-in-Publication Data

Waldrep, Kent.
    Fourth and long: the Kent Waldrep story / by Kent Waldrep and Susan Malone ; [foreword by Roger Staubach].
        p.   cm.
    ISBN 0-8245-1508-0
    1. Waldrep, Kent.   2. Football players—United States—Biography.
3. Paraplegics—United States—Biography.   4. Football players—Wounds and injuries.   5. Spinal cord—Wounds and injuries.
6. Texas Christian University—Football.   I. Malone, Susan.
II. Title.
GV939.W25A3   1996
796.332'092 B–dc20   95-13752
                                                                                                        CIP

To my family.
Their love is God's true blessing in my life.

— KENT

For Kent,
whose humor, integrity, and persistence opened my world.
Through Grace I not only came to work with you,
but to respect, trust, and love you.
Godspeed, my brother, on your quest.

— SUSAN

To Jay:
Hang in there pal.
A lot of good things
are right around the
corner!
God bless
Kent

CONTENTS

Part Three
*Hope is not optimism;
it is a state of the soul.*

ACKNOWLEDGMENTS

It is impossible for me to thank everyone who has touched my life with love and compassion. From board members and staff who have given generously of their money and hearts, to complete strangers who have written or prayed words of inspiration... my love goes out to all of you.

This book is written in the hopes of offering a source of encouragement to all of you who face your own Fourth and Long. By chronicling my adventure through the "Medical Twilight Zone," I hope you can identify with me and decide that your challenge in life can also be won, that you are important as a human being, and that you will leave your footprint for the future.

No matter what the Good Lord has in store for Kent Waldrep, this book will always be a reminder to my family and friends of my everlasting love. They have all sacrificed unselfishly toward my vision. I can only hope that we can look forward to many more years filled with the joy, laughter, crying together, learning experiences, little setbacks, and big successes that have molded us into such a loving family.

And... I promise to be better about my hair!

— KENT

And from both of us — a special thanks to our agent, Dick Smith, whose tireless efforts pulled together the publishing pieces.

9

FOREWORD

When I met Kent Waldrep five years after his injury, he sat in a wheelchair smiling. He seemed so fit that the more we talked, the more I expected him to stand up. And I sensed that although this man was confined to his chair, he didn't sit around much.

I'd known about Kent from following football at Texas Christian University and from all the news reports of his accident, his rehabilitation, and the trip to Russia for alternative treatments. I had always admired his courage. But it was not until I met and began working with him to help fund research for a paralysis cure that I came to understand the power of his persistence.

Kent Waldrep is a fighter. He got knocked down. Hard. And when you get knocked down, you either stay there, or you pick yourself up and fight some more. That is exactly what Kent has done. He refused to sit back and feel sorry for himself. Rather, he grasped the bull by the horns and has accomplished as much as any person possibly could — not just physically, but mentally as well — in order to make a difference and offer hope to millions in similar situations. Through actions more than words Kent says, "I've got a mission." What he has achieved on that mission is nothing short of phenomenal.

If a spinal injury occurs now, immediate treatments are given to halt more damage before paralysis becomes permanent. These treatments were not available in 1974 for Kent Waldrep. That they're accessible now can be traced to the awareness, fund-raising dollars, and scientific support propelled by Kent's persistence.

When Kent began his foundation, the hope for a paralysis cure was virtually nonexistent. By utilizing leadership capabilities, actuated through tenacity, he first mobilized the *idea* of a cure. With perseverance, he joined his own hopes and thoughts with those of everyone involved in this issue — scientific researchers, families of disabled persons, the general public. Kent Waldrep just would not quit. Nor will he, until a cure is found.

Although Kent's injury occurred while playing football, his greatest impact has been realized off the athletic field. The lessons learned through competition, however, have aided his quest. Sports teaches you not to quit, to be patient, to proceed. It instills the value of working *with* a team — utilizing each person's strengths while learning to trust yourself and others. Perhaps most important for the arena of life, sports teaches it is not the crisis that matters, but how you handle the crisis.

Life often presents us with the two-minute warning when, down by two touchdowns, we can either fold or dig down deeper to come back and make the winning play. It's our choice. Staring into the face of fourth and long, Kent always opts to fight on.

In 2 Corinthians 4:8–9 Paul speaks of perseverance backed by faith: "We are troubled on every side, yet not distressed; we are perplexed, but not in despair; persecuted, but not forsaken; cast down, but not destroyed."

In essence, we're all just temporal creatures; our only permanence is through our faith in the Almighty God. And though Kent's temporal life has been hampered, he doesn't blame that on God. Faith has simply reinforced Kent's steadfast resolve to deal with the problem.

Kent's belief in God has allowed him to be strong throughout his trials. People's faith is often firm when all is well, but when things go wrong it weakens. If faith is truly related to the permanence of salvation however, the toughest times will only temper us. The strongest steel does indeed pass through the flame.

Through grace and by faith, Kent marches forth.

Each and every one of us can make a difference in this life — if we *do* it. Kent's contribution will exceed that of most people. If he could have chosen this course, I doubt that he would have. But he was dealt a hand and has made the most of it. The point is Kent *does* it. He affects not only those who relate to his injury, but anyone dealing with life's problems. He is an inspiration to us all.

Kent's impact has already been significant. When everyone else focused on rehabilitation, when a cure wasn't even considered, Kent mobilized the funds to finance research. He initiated not only the *hope* for a cure, but its potential reality as well. He has kept society's awareness raised, research dollars accruing, and scientists motivated.

Hand-in-hand, these things turn the research machine's wheels. Kent is the catalyst that motivates that machine.

He has developed an unprecedented vehicle for driving paralysis studies. Whether by next year, the year after, or five years hence, Kent's commitment has caused the once inconceivable to be nearing reality. He has worked to make a difference not only for himself, but for so many others.

The *agape* side of life can prove difficult for all of us; often we do things expecting something in return. And though Kent began his quest for himself, he has now grown far beyond that. He *knows* the impact a cure will have on millions of folks.

People frequently impose their own limitations. But some abide by no such restrictions. As Kent often asks, what is impossible? Technological advances once thought preposterous are today taken for granted. Impossible merely identifies the limitations we place on ourselves.

I have been continually enriched by my friendship with Kent, honored to be associated with him, and inspired by his courage. Kent's story bolsters the faith within us all; it enlightens and uplifts. It constantly raises that question: *What is impossible?* For while heroism in athletic endeavor is calculable, in life true greatness is more subtle and filled with intangibles. But by whatever means you measure him, Kent Waldrep is a genuine hero.

— ROGER STAUBACH

Part One

What we call the beginning is often the end....
The end is where we start from.

— T. S. ELIOT

✧ CHAPTER ONE ✧

THE END OF ONE BEGINNING:
"RED RIGHT 28 ON SET"

"You _____ hofner asked, as
sunsl _____ iispering of realized _____ istian University
jogge _____ rd their dressing
room

Th _____ season, when two
Kent _____ teammates took
Wald _____ n Kent wouldn't
conf

"I _____ n anxious during
prega _____ TCU's opener six
week _____ Saturday against
Texas A&M, he played only one quarter, and this week he alternated
in practice with his back-up. For today's game in Birmingham, Coach
Shof had waited to decide which tailback would start. Until now.

"Well, it's yours. Have a good 'un," Shof said. Then the coach sped
up and disappeared among the other players.

The clear sunlight of an Alabama autumn afternoon shone brighter.
Crisp and clean, the cool air tickled his skin. What a perfect day for
football! And this day, especially, was every college player's dream —
to line up against Alabama's Crimson Tide, the number one team in
the country. Seventy thousand raucous fans filled the stadium. And
earlier as he jogged onto the field for warm-up, Kent's gaze immediately searched for a specific someone. Against the goal post and under
a hound's-tooth fedora stood the unmistakable frame of Paul "Bear"
Bryant.

Unbelievable, Kent had thought, simply unbelievable. This day truly

17

was the essence of football. He breezed through pregame stretches and maneuvers, though on one pass pattern he slipped and fell on his left knee. Damn, he'd thought, this surface is hard.

But the thought was fleeting.

A group of ten-year-old boys had been shagging field goals behind the uprights. When they approached Kent for his autograph, a smile teased across his full lips. These were the Kent Waldreps of tomorrow; they worshiped the sport. None cared that Kent belonged to the opposing team, but only that he was a college football player. It was a dream that Kent shared with the boys, and one he well understood.

Kent had grown up watching his own football heroes — the Texas Longhorns and the Dallas Cowboys. He imitated their athletic skills in front yard pick-up games. Quite often, those games consisted of Kent against Kent.

Decked-out in shoulder pads, jersey, and a Texas Longhorn helmet, he would huddle, call the play, run, and then tackle himself. Executing the pattern, he would also call the play-by-play, complete with crowd noise. In that yard his fantasy of playing big-time college football was born.

During today's warm-up, Kent felt an instant kinship with those boys seeking autographs. And here, now, he was about to realize his fifth-grade ambition. Now, if they could just hold Alabama to under fifty points.

The salty aroma of still-clean sweat filled the locker room. Rubbing alcohol and the pungent bite of liniment drifted through the quiet spaces. Only the ripping and tearing of adhesive tape sliced the silence. Players sat alone, checking gear, reviewing playbooks, thinking. The air inside lay heavy and still, as if the barometric pressure had plummeted before a tornado.

Kent inhaled the aromas of battle, accustomed to this bottled-up tension, as were the others. When they emerged from the tunnel and hit the field, this energy would explode into a whirling funnel fueled by adrenaline and nerve. But for now, the eerie quiet.

Precise attention to detail earmarked Kent's pregame routine. He inspected every piece of his uniform, insuring an impeccable appearance.

First, he tied and taped his shoelaces. The tape around his shoes looked tough on television. He applied zinc oxide below his eyes. The black war paint reduced the glare of the sun. It also enhanced the gladiator-like image.

Finally, he meticulously tucked in his jersey, hoisted his socks to just below the kneecap, and adjusted hip and arm pads to a comfortable fitting. All was perfect.

And just in time. Coach Shof readied for one last desperate attempt to convince them they actually had a prayer of beating the number one team in the country. I, too, am the eternal optimist, Kent thought. TCU's chances, however, rivaled those of General Custer. But the game *was* with Alabama, and that alone provided enough inspiration to pump up a stone statue.

Shof, pursing his lips, began his standard pep talk — which had failed to gain inclusion in any motivational tapes.

Kent ran fingers through his dark hair and grinned to himself. Though he loved Shof, he, like his teammates, played hard and wanted to win for the coach because Shof cared for them as individuals. Not all coaches did, and Kent had played for both kinds. Shof was honest and a Christian, with a great mind for offensive schemes and game plans. But he was a quiet man, even-tempered, demanding though not exactly inspiring.

So as the coach delivered his version of Zig Ziglar, Kent thought of how the pep talk ought to go:

> Gentlemen, the oddsmakers have predicted a reenactment of the battle of Little Big Horn. And I must admit, you will fight this war on your own. Because I'll be cheering from the protection of the sidelines!
>
> No, seriously, men, we have a great challenge before us today. The outcome will not alter the course of world peace, but how you handle this adversity may help determine the content of your character.
>
> Now, if Coach Bryant becomes ill; if Richard Todd throws six interceptions; if Ozzie Newsome doesn't catch a pass; if Tony Nathan fumbles five times; if Woodrow Lowe does not make one tackle; and if we somehow figure a way to score, then, men, we might pull an upset!
>
> Now, let's join together and pray *hard* all those things happen!

That, Kent thought, would loosen us up. As Shof continued, Kent imagined the Alabama locker room. Bear Bryant was a legend for many reasons: the second most wins ever by a college coach, numerous national championships, bowl games every year, conference titles, and the personal aspects of that hat and gruff voice. His players respected him, however, because though the Bear was *tough*, he cared.

Kent recalled one of a litany of famous stories about the man. During August drills in the Texas heat, while Coach Bryant struggled to rebuild Texas A&M's losing football program, some players were said to have snuck out in the night and hitchhiked hundreds of miles back to the safety of civilization to escape sheer hell on earth. The Bear's training camp made boot camp look like a YMCA retreat.

He imagined the Bear's gruff voice speaking to his players:

> Boys, you have everything to lose and nothing to gain against these TCU boys. You can go through the motions and still win, or you can make your mamas and papas proud and play to your full potential.
>
> Life's gonna offer you these same choices, and now's as good a time as any to make the right one.
>
> Now, go out there and hit them boys and knock 'em down; help 'em up; then tell 'em you'll be right back.

Kent imagined those players pouring from the dressing room, ready to defend their "'Bama Pride" to the death. The bookmaker's line of TCU plus 35 might be hard to defend. Shof clapped. Kent rechecked his uniform, then smoothed his perfectly placed hair.

The teams fired onto the field and all else dimmed but the kickoff. Kent fidgeted on the sidelines, adjusting pads, retucking his jersey. The packed stadium roared like the freight train vibrations of a tornado thundering through. Kent bit at his fingernails and wiped sweaty palms on the back of his britches. He wanted the ball.

This hadn't exactly been his banner season. Before breaking his collarbone, he'd torn a calf muscle and broken his right hand during preseason drills. Now, finally, came his chance to prove himself.

The game progressed, and they held their own. Kent had several carries, gaining five or six yards each time — a good average for any tailback. But the team couldn't seem to sustain a drive as the first quarter ended with Alabama leading 7–0.

Still, they were in the game as the second quarter began. Neither team mounted much of a threat, and the momentum stayed up for grabs. With eight minutes left in the half, TCU took possession on their own twenty-five-yard line.

Kent darted up the middle for seven yards. Quarterback Lee Cook completed two passes. Mike Luttrell, TCU's All-American fullback, ran inside, gaining two tough yards. The Frogs were in Alabama territory.

Then came a quick screen pass and Kent almost broke for big yardage down the sideline, possibly a touchdown. But the Crimson Tide defense overcame Kent's blockers and knocked him out of bounds. Nevertheless, he gained nine yards. First down.

Close. Close now. Adrenaline shut out all sounds, as always when he stepped on the field. And today Kent's instincts hit right on target. He sensed a big play; a hole about to open for him to surge through; big yards; maybe all the way. His faculties felt primed, reflexes ready, muscles pumped. He adjusted his helmet for the fortieth time.

Mike Renfro ran in from the sideline with the play, relaying it to Lee Cook. Lee repeated the call in the huddle.

"Red Right 28 on Set. And Abe, Coach said get outside — quick," Lee added.

Good deal, Kent thought, an end sweep. Get outside quick. Our pressbox coaches must have spotted a weakness in 'Bama's outside pursuit. If the execution went as planned, Kent's 4.5-second-40 speed on his six-foot, 185-pound frame could turn the corner quickly enough to break for another first down. Every beat of his heart pumped "quick-outside, quick-outside." He sensed himself exploding from his stance. Step back then right for the pitch from Lee. His instincts would take it from there. He wiped sweaty palms against his britches.

The huddle broke. Kent inserted his mouthpiece. He took position in the backfield, behind the left guard. Though he would charge to 'Bama's left side, he glanced right, then left, then front — as always — to keep the defense guessing. He grabbed his face mask and adjusted his helmet.

Lee stood over center, surveying the defensive scheme. He could audible and call an alternate play, but only if the designated one stood no chance against the defensive alignment. All offensive players took their stances. "DOWN!" Lee barked.

"Down" was the first word in their sequence to snap the ball. No movement, Kent thought. Don't anticipate the count. Then explode. Back and right. Take the pitch. Tuck the ball. Look for blockers. Hope for blockers. Pray for more blockers than defensive players. Back and right. The thoughts swept simultaneously through Kent's mind.

"Set" was the designated snap count for this play — the next word in the sequence.

Kent waited. His entire body tightened like a compressed coil.

"Set!"

Every muscle exploded in a coordinated movement to his right, in perfect position for the pitch from Lee.

Two steps into the motion, Kent caught the ball. He accelerated around his right end. Surging, he caught the pulling guard and tackle.

'Round the corner, a red sea of jerseys spread like a wall. The play had not fooled the defense.

In that split second he thought, buckle up. Juking one defender to set up a block, his lowered shoulder met the next.

The Alabama pursuit caught up. Momentum propelled him forward. A boom lowered to his left side. Kent and a wad of players hurdled toward the Alabama bench.

Suddenly, a downed 'Bama player looked up. He scuttled sideways. A roll-block blasted into Kent's legs from behind. Along with the trio of tacklers, Kent became airborne.

I've done this before, he thought. The turf surged up to greet them. I'm gonna hit on my head. Like hundreds of other times.

Whomp!

I am standing on my head. Hours passed. His body fell gently, slowly, as a feather floats with no breeze to earth, then landed in a prone position on the field. There was no crash. No pain. No thud. There was nothing.

Through a haze of pink elephants and stars, he felt apart from his body, as if seeing someone else. Boy, has my bell been rung this time.

22

Get up. Get to the sideline. Why won't my legs move? Get your dizzy ass to the bench!

Breath wouldn't come. Voices filled the air. Kent recognized the sounds of Elmer Brown, TCU's head trainer, and Sully, Elmer's assistant, though he couldn't bring their faces into focus. He kept trying to breathe. "Don't move your head!" Sully ordered.

"Can you feel this?" Elmer asked. "How about here?"

"Can you raise your right leg? How about your left? Move this foot! Cross your arms! Any feeling here? Don't move your head!"

Breathe, Kent thought. When your brain recovers, your legs will remember how to guide your body to the bench. Get this helmet off! I need oxygen, he tried to scream. No words emerged. Suffocating.

Panic.

Finally he gasped, "I can't breathe!"

A woman's voice sounded from behind his head. "Don't take that helmet off," she commanded.

A distant voice responded, "We have to give him mouth-to-mouth!"

"No," she replied firmly, calmly. "Cut the mouthpiece out."

"Hold his helmet still!" Sully ordered.

His helmet was grasped, steadily, gently. Suffocating.

Again Kent managed, "Get my helmet off! I can't breathe!"

"Listen to me," the woman said.

Wheezing, he pled, "I can't breathe."

"Yes, you can," she replied evenly. "Use your stomach muscles to breathe with. You're using them to talk. Now, push out with your stomach. There. Good. Now again."

The others sounded as if from a distance — a fuzzy hum. But this woman's voice was intense and sharp. Or was she an angel? Another echoed clearly and close, as if from within his mind. Through the haze and the chaos and clamoring din, a warm peace enveloped his body. God enfolded him. And he breathed.

Then, *shit*, the pain! Through his neck and shoulders shot a stabbing agony, as if a hundred knives plunged into his neck. His muscles were ripping apart. The pain blasted upward and exploded out through his head.

A thousand years passed. Backboard stretchers appeared. No use. Finally, a collapsible stretcher arrived. Orders fired amid a sea of blurred faces met Kent's consciousness as unknown arms positioned him onto a cart-like tractor. Slowly, so slowly, that cart crawled down the sidelines.

The tractor's roaring droned out the thousands and thousands of shouting voices that had been so clear, so crisp, in the autumn afternoon.

The woman continued to cradle his head. She spoke serenely, encouraging him to breathe, though Kent couldn't quite catch her words. But he breathed.

Bright sunlight switched to cooling shade as the cart left the field and entered the protected area under the east end zone bleachers.

A familiar voice asked, "What is your parents' phone number?"

"What?"

"We need to contact your parents."

"Take my helmet off," Kent pleaded for what felt like the fiftieth time.

"What is your parents' phone number?"

This is a joke, he thought. I'm somewhat distracted right now. I can't breathe, a shooting pain's exploding out the back of my neck, and some joker wants me to recite phone numbers. Now how am I supposed to do that? "We need to contact your parents."

To his own astonishment, Kent recited the number. The woman, who had never loosened her grip on Kent's helmet, positioned herself behind him in the ambulance. TCU's team physician, Dr. Eteir, sat on Kent's right, grasping a limp arm.

"Drive slowly," the sweet voice behind him said. "Slower than you've ever driven before."

We're in a turtle marathon, Kent deduced, pain searing across his neck, bursting open his head. Please, God, *please* let me pass out.

For the first time, he felt the woman's hands shake, ever so slightly. Man, she's been gripping my helmet for a long, long time. The strain must be killing her.

"Don't be scared," Kent assured her. "I'll be fine."

"Don't talk, sweetheart," she whispered. "I know you'll be fine."

Her words, soft and loving, lulled him into merciful blackness.

✧ CHAPTER TWO ✧

SURVIVING

Kent's eyes opened to a flood of lights. Bright, blinding, the white-hot glared like spotlights, as if illuminating a stage. Strange faces danced into and out of his line of vision. Sterile though caustic smells stung his senses. The clank of metal tormented his ears. And people poked him from all sides. Ah, he thought, the hospital.

Son-of-a-bitch! My neck! My shoulders! Why the hell don't these white-coated medicine men give me *something* for the pain?

"Can you hear me?" A doctor asked.

It ain't my hearing, Doc, it's my neck that's killing me. But he answered politely, "Yes, I'm fine, but my neck hurts quite a bit."

"We know. But we can't give you anything for the pain right now."

Not good news, Kent thought.

"We need to shave your head," the doctor said. "It's necessary so that we can put your head and neck into traction."

Kent's eyes darted wildly. What the hell? They want to shave my head cause my neck hurts? With tears welling up, he asked, "Why my hair?"

"It's necessary for the procedure."

Not my hair, he pled silently. Anything but my hair — my biggest obsession. In the heat of summer he sometimes showered three times a day in order to keep his hair in perfect place. Now these strange doctors had nonchalantly decided to Telly Savalas his head. *Fat chance.*

"No way you're shaving my head."

Several white-coats quietly reaffirmed, "We are going to shave your head."

Just then, two young and fresh faces appeared — a nurse for either side. Both gently stroked his forehead while reemphasizing the haircut's necessity. A clever tactic, Kent thought. Who here knew he was a sucker for pretty ladies? Though he still protested the shearing, the

25

nurses' gentle touches, their motherly reassurances, accomplished the madmen's objective.

With every hair that fell to the sheets, a tear followed. Okay, so I'm hurt bad, Kent reasoned, but why my hair? And where were Elmer and Sully?

The crazed hairdresser finished, and the doctor began again.

"We're now going to deaden your head so that the application of traction will be less painful."

Kent stared straight up. Thanks for the notice, Doc, but you guys are gonna do whatever you want anyway. Just get on with the show.

He rolled his eyes to either side. Completely prone, head held firmly in place, he couldn't see diddly-squat save what was directly above his face. This left a lovely view of the white ceiling.

Ouw! that feels like a needle sticking my head. Tiny pricks, into my head! They're deadening my skull when my neck is torturing me and then saying no pain medication. This place is a zoo!

"We are beginning the traction procedure," the doctor said. "You might experience some discomfort."

The nurses manned their battle stations beside his head.

The doctor announced, "We're beginning."

A drill started buzzing. What? Warning! Warning! his skull shouted. Help! Some dumb shit's drilling holes in my head! His skull kept screaming as the drill bored through. Some discomfort? He's killing me! A tidal wave of pain and terror engulfed him.

Kent knew his usually sleepy eyes had grown into huge hazel marbles. The nurses fondled his forehead again, murmuring assurances. All would be fine, they said. Just fine.

This time he didn't buy it. Why the drilling? he tried to cry out. What's inside my head that you witch doctors wanna look at? What in the devil was going on here?

But maybe it'll get me out of this godforsaken place and back home as soon as possible. After all, the thoughts floated to him, I have weekend plans with Katie. And a golf game scheduled that should generate much-needed extra cash.

The wildcatter act ceased after equal drilling had been completed above each ear. Kent sighed a little too soon.

The doctor reached back into his medieval bag of tricks. He applied

26

a screw and bolt to each hole, joining them with a wire. To that he attached a forty-pound weight, which pulled Kent's head firmly back.

A gaggle of medical faces appeared above him. Finally, Kent thought. Then the head quack announced, "We need to check the position of your shoulders and neck to assure correct alignment for the traction. This will require some pulling of your shoulders," he paused and then added, "to lower them for an X-ray of the spinal column."

Why are you consulting me? Kent questioned silently. Why solicit my response? It's clear my vote carries as much weight as one for Richard Nixon ultimately did. "Okay," he answered.

Each of the doctors pulled an arm. Coupled with the weight tugging his skull backward, this torture had Kent praying once more to pass out.

Son-of-a-bitch! he screamed again silently, though he uttered only loud moans. Seconds passed as minutes, minutes as hours. After an eternity, the cameraman gleaned the photographic evidence needed. The fiends were almost finished. But not before Kent's porch light flipped off. Pain relief had finally come.

The sun is shining on a lazy Saturday in Manhattan, where Kent's parents live. Denise Waldrep stands by her sink, washing lunch dishes. Her husband, Al, sits comfortably, watching a college football game and joking with her. Halftime comes and the Alabama-TCU score flashes up. Al calls that the score is 14–3. They decide Kent must be having a good game since Alabama led by so little. All is well. And after the game is over, she and Al are going for a walk in the sunshine. Having their three children grown and out of the house has left them with something of a second honeymoon.

The phone rings. As she says hello, a man asks to speak with Mr. Waldrep. Al picks up, then his face ties together like the stitching on a rag-doll. Denise can tell from Al's responses that the call is from Alabama. Her heart stops. Something is wrong with Kent.

Her mind becomes foggy from the butterscotch rays of the sun that pour through the west window. Al finishes his conversation and hangs up the phone. He speaks to her of the call, but though Denise tries, she cannot understand his words.

27

"Pack a suitcase," Al says.

Denise packs but cannot focus. She feels as if split, two people in one body, the one packing and the other standing off to the side, watching. She dresses and they catch a cab to the airport. Neither had checked the flights.

Al places her in a seat, setting the suitcase down beside her. "Sit here," he says, "while I see about a flight." His voice comes from somewhere far away, but Denise sits. She watches him walk from the ticket counter to the pay phones, then back again. He is calling Alabama, she thinks in a lucid moment, though whether it is the she in-the-body or the she to-the-side who has this thought, Denise is not certain.

After an eternity of hours, Al takes her to board the plane. Where is Birmingham? she wonders. How long will it take this silver vessel to get there?

Not many others board, and after take-off the stewardess gives Al the okay to pace the aisles. His legs cramp when he is nervous, Denise thinks. She watches him pace. The others talk and laugh and from her other-world, none of it makes sense.

Denise touches the suitcase tucked under the seat. Feeling it reassures her. She remembers Al saying he has given permission for traction, and the vision of Kent's arms and legs hanging in the air from funny-looking straps fills her mind. How miserable her boy would be, confined like that. How tortured.

The plane floats down and Al propels her up the jetway. Three men await their arrival. One wears a TCU purple blazer. *Dear God.* Denise's knees buckle, and Al grabs her before she crashes to the hard, cold linoleum.

But she hears the men introduced as the chancellor of TCU, a public relations man from University Hospital, and Sully, TCU's assistant trainer.

Kent is in good hands, they say. The best. University Hospital in the University of Alabama Medical Center. Prepared. The hospital is prepared for such cases. All the expertise. Top-rated medical staff. Caring professionals. They might as well have been speaking Russian, but Denise catches enough. Enough for her heart once more to quit beating, then jarringly restart.

28

In the emergency room, Kent Waldrep's eyes opened. His escape into the painless unconscious had ended. As his gaze focused, a pleasant and familiar though startling face became distinct.

It couldn't be, he thought. It is. No, not possible.

But it was. Framed like an angel against the bright white backdrop of the E.R. ceiling stood Katie.

Kent said, "I'm either dreaming, hallucinating, or I've died and gone to heaven."

Katie leaned down and kissed him. "Are you dreaming or dead?" she asked.

"What? Where did you — "

"Hush. Be quiet now," she said softly. "I was listening to the game and when they said you were taken to the hospital, I thought you might like some company. And," she added, flashing her famous grin, "I brought your clean clothes."

Kent stared at the grin that had melted his heart from the get-go. Katie's shoulder-length dark hair, big brown eyes, and beautiful, fragile features had, in the two months they had dated, caused him to float into a spiral of love. And, as usual, he was unusually insecure about the relationship.

Looking at her now, at the plump, smiling lips, Kent had never been so in love. Oh, she wasn't his first. He had dated one girl at TCU for a year and a half. When she dumped him — his first real dump, and for not nearly as good-looking a guy — he was crushed. Even today, he was still somewhat in love with that girl.

He had also fallen in love the previous summer with another. He met Terry Stanford on a blind double date. Though not out with each other, both felt an immediate attraction. When autumn arrived and they attended different universities, they remained in touch as friends.

With the innocence of youth, Kent loved completely. But now, leaning over him smiled Katie, reassuring. She spoke of how God's strength and love would get him through. Her strong faith soothed his soul.

This, Kent thought, is what those witch doctors *should* have ordered.

He dozed in and out. Faces appeared over him. Sometimes they spoke. Sometimes he answered. All was a fog.

29

Coach Shofner arrived. Kent thought how strong and handsome Shof looked, short dark hair framing that chiseled face. The coach spoke in his low, quiet voice. Kent asked, "How'd the game come out?"

Shof told him, but Kent forgot. Forty-one to something. Something to three. What was the final score? he wondered again.

He awoke in a smaller room. The ceiling looked different, and, with peripheral vision, he could see walls. He hadn't seen walls in the E.R.

Voices, familiar voices, filled the room. He braced, his mind refusing to function. But with a jolt he recognized those voices. They belonged to his mom and dad.

Entering the hospital, Denise Waldrep recognizes several other people from TCU, and Kent's girlfriend, Katie. I have never met her, Denise thinks, but that is Katie. Then she follows Al into the doctor's office.

Her mind begins to latch onto things.

Kent has crushed his fifth cervical vertebra. He is having trouble breathing. The doctor will operate. He will fuse the fourth, fifth and sixth vertebrae, and rebuild the fifth with bone from Kent's hip.

Can't breathe, Denise thought. My boy cannot breathe. Well, make him breathe.

"He may not make it through surgery," the doctor repeats. He has said this many times. The thought will not lodge in Denise's brain. "Do you want him put on a respirator?"

"No," Al answers. Denise hears this but cannot comprehend. She turns a savage glare onto her husband.

"Honey," Al begins, so oddly coherent, "Kent and I have had this conversation many times. We both agreed if the time ever came, we'd take care of each other this way." He is patting her forearm as he speaks. His other arm surrounds her shoulders. His eyes are so full of concern, and some of that concern is for her.

Dr. Galbraith is nodding at Al.

Denise looks from one to the other. "Kent will come out of the surgery just fine," she hears herself say.

They both stare at her, and then Dr. Galbraith rises. "You can see Kent before surgery," he says.

Down the hall, the sterile, white hall, they follow the doctor. Into a small, cold room, Denise walks to see her son being prepared for surgery.

His gladiator gear has been removed, down to his taped ankles. His head is three-quarters shaven. A metal bonnet with wires and screws attaches from one ear to another. Dried blood is still caked around the traction. Dried blood on the sheets. Her son's flaccid arms lie at his sides, IVs hooked up to both. A catheter tube snakes out from under the flimsy sheet to a drainage bag hanging under the bed.

This cannot be her son. Her son, so meticulous about his appearance, so fussy about his hair. The horror of it sucks the air from her lungs.

Denise and Al both try to smile. All will be fine, they say.

Kent grins up at his dad and says, "My hair short enough for you now, Dad?"

Al smiles and nods, then turns away and Denise fills Kent's line of vision, speaking in low and comforting tones while Al weeps to the wall so his son will not see.

Then they are ushered from the room.

Denise motions to one of the nurses. "Kent has his contacts in," she says, though having no clue as to where that fact came from.

"We'll take care of it," the nurse assures her. Then they are taken to a small office to wait out the surgery.

Denise keeps seeing Kent's hair. Al never let the boy grow it long, at least not while they lived within driving distance. But after his parents moved out of state — this very year — Kent let it grow out a bit. Then some friends sent a TCU football program to Denise and Al. A photo of Kent with semi-long hair sent Al into a fit. More than one long distance call was made, explaining to Kent in no uncertain terms his father's thoughts on that hair. And now, it is gone.

Time moves in slow motion. The little room is crowded, and Denise, a generally gregarious woman, wants to be left alone. The part of her that has broken off and is watching wonders why she does not want a cigarette, but she does not. Al stays on the phone, keeping callers abreast of Kent's condition, keeping family members posted.

This Katie person has Kent's clean clothes for his trip home. Denise is oddly irritated by this. But more so as it seems every few seconds

31

Katie breaks out with a "Praise the Lord!" This works on Denise's mind like Chinese water torture.

Finally, a nurse enters and says Kent is being taken to recovery and Denise and Al can see him for a few minutes. They meet Kent and his escort team in the hallway.

Kent looks alert and says, "Dad, I'll be fine. And we'll play golf real soon." As the entourage moves down the hall, Denise and Al melt into tears, and into one another.

Other arms come to comfort, and a nurse informs them they cannot see Kent again until the next day. While he is in ICU, they can see him for fifteen minutes every four hours.

They are taken to a motel. Denise notices it is 3:00 a.m. The room is filled with flowers, all kinds of flowers sent by friends and Alabama fans. Al cannot bear them — they remind him of a funeral and he cannot breathe. Finally, they set the flowers outside the motel door.

Denise opens the suitcase for nightclothes. The suitcase, so carefully carried and watched over, is empty. No clothes, no toothbrush, no nothing. She forgot to pack.

Throughout the hours of darkness, they repeat to one another, "If he makes it through this night, he will be fine." And they speak of mundane things.

As the sun peeps over the horizon, Al's sister, Wanda, Denise's friend Mildred Walker, and the Waldreps' youngest daughter, Terry Lynn, and her boyfriend, Brad — a best friend of Kent's — arrive. Terry Lynn and Kent are close, both in relationship and age. Only fourteen months apart, they have grown up and experienced life in the same time frame, sharing as only siblings can. Denise knows Kent's sister's presence will boost his spirits.

More tears flow with the full disclosure of the injury, and now something new. In the brutal light of morning, the gravity of the tragedy takes hold. Kent could die.

By 6:00 a.m. the group is back at the hospital and sequestered in a private meeting room to wait, watch the clock, make phone calls (the chancellor of TCU has given Al his telephone credit card in order to keep the family posted), watch, and wait some more. Every four hours they have fifteen minutes with their son.

He is dopey, mostly sleeping, positioned on a striker frame and still in traction, hooked up to all sorts of tubes and machinery.

The sight is almost more than a mother can bear. But she does. She prays, hoping with each allotted time that he will be more alert, more talkative, that the doctors will become positive about his recovery.

Sunday drifts into Monday, a haze of fifteen-minute sabbaticals. Family friends Tuck and Bobby Blanchard drive over. They heard the news while in Tennessee on vacation. The Waldreps' oldest daughter, Carole, arrives by seventeen-hour bus ride, and now the immediate family is complete, the unit melding together to supply one another — and Kent — with courage. Most of each day is spent with everyone reassuring one another that all will work out.

Alabama Governor George Wallace calls to say that Kent has the finest doctors in the world. These are the same doctors and staff members who cared for him after a gunshot left him paralyzed. This, too, is a comfort. More friends, the Pettigrews, arrive on Tuesday bringing Al and Denise a change of clothes. So many friends.

The hospital staff is wonderful. The family is overwhelmed by the sheer numbers of calls coming in, flowers, wires, and letters expressing best wishes and hope. Coach Shofner has stayed, dying a little each day. Barbara McClary, the nurse who had held Kent's head on the field and to the hospital, visits often. And Bear Bryant has come both evenings.

It is an awesome sight to see the Bear stroll down the hall. Denise feels the man's presence, long before she sees him. The gruffness in his voice is filled with such concern.

Tuesday dawns a bit brighter. Kent is moved out of ICU and into a private room. Nurses remain posted, but the family can stay with him constantly too. Having Kent in a room where we all can touch him will make him well, Denise senses without actually thinking it. She believes in miracles, in faith being the evidence of things not seen. In slow stages, her fog begins to lift. And the two women she had split into merge, once more, into one.

Finally, Kent thought, out of ICU and into a private room. His experience after surgery had not exactly been a stroll on the golf course.

Thank God, most of it was foggy. He remembered the screams and moans surrounding him, the loneliness, the cold. For tiny patches of time, his family and Katie and friends were allowed to come "view the body."

Mainly he remembered seeing legs and feet as most of his time was spent upside down, looking at the floor. And of course, he recalls the demons. He'd never gotten along with pain medication, and the massive doses now prescribed created monstrous hallucinations. He constantly fought these beasts in his mind. When he had wanted the medication upon first arriving, the staff denied it. He later overheard this was because they didn't expect him to make it and wanted him lucid if his parents got there in time.

But now a real step forward. In the private room, all his family, friends, and Katie would be close to boost his recovery. And finally some quiet. No more screams and moans.

Not again! No sooner had he gotten into his room, than the screeching clatter of jackhammers pounding through concrete just down the hall replaced the sounds of human cries.

I just don't believe it, he thought. Here I am, fresh out of ICU, fighting for my life, seeking a little peace and quiet, and these bozos are tearing down the hospital around me. No respect. I get no respect.

The traction wiring attached to his head picked up *every* vibration of the jackhammers like a telegraph. This provided a constant clanging in his ears as it blasted into his mind.

But his parents soon had him moved to another room, and acute rehabilitation began. Everything was new — all basic human processes had to be learned a different way.

Being fed on his back was a neat trick. One of the first nurses almost choked him when she shoved down a piece of lettuce with the mashed potatoes. Adept maneuvers by the staff freed the obstruction, but didn't prevent the wrath of Denise and Al. The nurse received her walking papers.

"Hey," Kent asked to no one in particular, "got any of those for me?"

But rehab progressed. He visited with family, read the Bible with Katie, and learned more medical terminology than he ever wanted to know. Probably the worst part was being turned over every four hours.

"Not again," Kent said as the nurse came to flip his bed.

He had been lying on his back, but obviously that luxury was over. Gotta stay ahead of those pressure sores. So every four hours they flipped him, face down, to study the lines on the floor.

His circular electric bed differed from the striker frame in that it flipped over vertically rather than horizontally. It had been dizzying at first, like revolving inside a carnival ride on an stomach full of cotton-candy. But the dizziness wasn't as bad as the supine position itself. Though this did relieve stress on his body elsewhere, it thrust intense pressure to his forehead and chin. And the hospital floor wasn't his favorite view.

"How's my best sweetheart," a woman asked.

It was Barbara McClary, Kent knew, though he couldn't see her face. She visited often, her presence easing his heart as it did the day of the accident. But today, he couldn't muster a smile.

"Hi," he answered.

"I see they have you staring at the floor on schedule," she said brightly.

All at once, he started crying. Hard.

"I want outa here," he sobbed. "Just let me die."

Barbara's fingers smoothed instantly down his cheek. As he continued to cry, she murmured softly. That same calm spread over him — as it had on the football field.

"I'm sorry," he said finally.

"Blow," Barbara said, holding a tissue to his nose. She wiped his eyes and sat so he could look into her face. Yes, he thought, God's angel.

"I'm sorry," he repeated. "It's just my agony talking."

"You're allowed," she answered. "You get to be afraid."

"I don't really want to die."

Barbara said softly, "I know."

They talked for a long while, and the knots within him eased.

Before she left, he said, "Please don't tell anyone I said those things. I don't want Mom and Dad to worry."

"I won't," she answered. "They keep saying how your faith and optimism keep all their spirits up. But Kent," Barbara paused then added, "you can cry to me anytime."

Thank you, God, Kent prayed. Thank you for Barbara. Thank you.

After yet another flipping, Terry Lynn breezed in saying cheerfully,

"Mail Call!" She positioned her skinny self cross-legged on the floor, not far from his face. In her arms bulged the day's mail, the bundle dwarfing her. These visits with all the cards and telegrams were Kent's saving grace when he stared at the floor, though usually the sentiments made everyone cry.

Terry Lynn started sorting through and reading cards. Her lilting voice and sweet, pretty face eased Kent's mind. Notes from all over the country had come, one from Mr. and Mrs. Nolan Ryan. Notes from other celebrities, family and friends, and rhymes from elementary school children spilled onto the floor. Some were to Al and Denise, and Terry Lynn sorted them into a separate pile.

"Oh, here's one from Ruth and John Winn," she began before setting it down. The Winns were old family friends. Kent went steady with their daughter, Juanita, in the sixth and seventh grades. "It says, 'He has always been our favorite and we love him dearly. Our thoughts and prayers are with all of you.'"

Kent smiled, though he had to swallow hard.

"And here's one from Tricia!" Tricia was Denise's best friend from the El Paso days — where the family lived when Kent was three through seven.

Terry started reading,

> Kent darling,
>
> Hope this finds you feeling better today —
>
> We think about you so much and what a sweet, brave young man you are. You hang in there, and know everyone in El Paso is pulling for you. We've had so many phone calls. I talked to Jerry Wright's mother this morning and she had heard about your accident on the radio. It seems like the entire state of Texas is praying for you. Kent, I don't know why this had to happen to you, but you'll lick it, of this we have no doubt. Take care, sweetheart —
>
> Love, Tricia

Terry's voice had begun to break, and now she sat crying, leaning to one side to miss the flood of tears streaming from Kent's eyes. For a time they sat, faces inches apart, and wept.

Finally, both sets of tears slowed and Kent winked.

"How about a Kleenex?" he asked. "I'm drowning here." Terry giggled. "I'd hate to have that be the cause of your death after all this."

"It'd be on *your* conscience," he said and laughed.

Through more giggles and grins, Terry wiped Kent's eyes and nose. Then for hours she read. They constantly laughed through the school kids' attempts to rhyme words with "spines" and "backs." One went:

> Sorry to hear
> You hit on your head.
> But be a good boy
> And get out of bed!

Finally, the nurse came to flip the bed back and Kent again lay right side up.

As Terry Lynn left, Dr. Shirley, the urologist, walked briskly into the room.

"How you doing, stud?" he asked.

"Ready to rock 'n' roll," Kent answered. "Provided my plumbing's working."

"Well, let's see what my trusty old roto-rooter might do today," Dr. Shirley said, beginning his work. "You know," he began, "I've drilled wells for all kinds of folks — young, old, fat, skinny, mean, funny. Yeah, just about all kinds. And you know what they all have in common?"

"What?" Kent asked, biting the bait.

"At some point they all find a way to surprise me during this procedure and *piss* all over me. Like you just did!"

Kent chuckled and then said, "Yeah, well, at least we're honest about it. I know people who'll piss on your back and tell you it's raining."

Dr. Shirley nodded, grinning.

The man was a godsend. Actually, he was Kent's goal line, dressed in white — his game's winning touchdown.

A broken neck received from a water-skiing accident had left Dr. Shirley paralyzed from the shoulders down. Now the man was whole again.

37

Kent knew, in every cell of his being, that he, too, would walk and work and be whole, just like Dr. Shirley.

The urologist finished and left, right before Dr. Galbraith and his flock of eager-to-shine interns entered. They poked and prodded and checked reflexes. This, along with the bloodletting routine, wasn't Kent's favorite part of the day. Besides, he needed the blood more than they needed to test it. Hell's bells, the color looked good and there seemed an ample supply, though it *had* to be dwindling.

He drifted off again. When he awoke, it was to the unmistakable presence of Coach Bryant.

Coach Bryant had with him two special visitors — George Steinbrenner of the New York Yankees and Charlie Finley of the World Champion Oakland A's.

Through his awe, Kent thought, I must look like absolute hell. And in front of *these* guys, too.

Coach Bryant broke the ice. "Kent," he began, "you know we've enjoyed you hanging around here. But it's time for you to quit lying around loafing and get back to TCU." The trace of a grin graced his grizzled face.

With as strong a voice as he could muster, Kent answered, "That's my plan, Coach."

Steinbrenner and Finley each presented Kent with an autographed baseball. They wished him a speedy recovery, then left Kent and Coach Bryant alone. Again, Coach Bryant spoke first.

"I want you to know, Kent, you've already made us all proud."

"Sir," Kent began, "it was a privilege to have played against your team."

Coach Bryant nodded. "You've touched a lot of folks here in Alabama. Everyone appreciates your spirit and wants to help. I want you to know that I'll always be here for you. You're one of my boys now, and together we'll beat this thing and get you back on your feet."

Swallowing hard to choke down the tears, Kent put on his best game face. "Coach," he began, paused, and then said with all the strength he could muster, "I promise you I'll always give 110 percent."

"I know, son," the gruff voice responded. "But you call me whenever you need to talk to a friend. Anytime, home or office. Now, you tell these doctors to fix you up and get you home. And I'll be back to see you."

As the coach turned to go, Kent said, "It's rumored that you have a direct line to heaven."

"No," the Bear answered softly, "I just get telegrams through."

"Send one for me?"

"It's already done." And with that, he left.

Kent watched as the broad shoulders disappeared from the room and sensed an energy had just left. But it felt as if some of the energy remained, a gift from the man in that fedora.

Kent slept fitfully that night, as usual.

The next day dawned, and the routine began anew. About mid-morning, in bounced Karen, his physical therapist.

"Ready to work?" she asked cheerfully. She reminded Kent of a true-life southern belle. As they proceeded through the range-of-motion exercises, her encouragement never waned.

The movements felt good. Kent had feeling in his upper body, so the bicep curls and circular motion relieved the constant cramps in his shoulders and neck. Both hands tingled with a numbly dulled sensation, as if he were being pricked by dozens of needles without any sharpness. But when Karen worked his legs, lifting and then bending the knees and ankles, he detected no sensation. His lower limbs felt like foreign objects belonging to someone, or something, else. Though scared, Kent kept his fear to himself. After all, it was just a matter of time.

And time moved slowly. The nights were the worst. Though Denise or Al stayed with him almost constantly, they did concede to friends and spent late nights and early mornings at the motel.

For Kent, sleep did not come easy. The traction constantly irritated his neck, and his shoulders cramped due to lack of movement. His pillow was little more than a washcloth, as any excess movement or elevation of his neck had to be restrained.

So during those long, sleepless hours, he thought of moving his arms and legs. He concentrated for hours on flexing his biceps, then on wiggling his toes, progressing up to bending his knees.

39

To a person whose entire life had been spent in sports, relying on a body that had performed perfectly since childhood *on its own,* this conscious direction to finely honed muscles was like learning a foreign language.

After the initial panic had come severe frustration. Existing only from the shoulders up made him crazy. But when the feeling came back, so surely would the movement. And though his legs wouldn't respond, they were still very large and muscular, causing him to feel somewhat secure. All in all, though, he felt like a twenty-year-old corpse, his head being the only part that functioned.

Kent had competed all his life. By second grade, he was swimming competitively, never to be beaten. The local coach had wanted to train him through junior high school, and on to Nationals. But Kent viewed swimming as simply a summer ritual, something to pass the time until Little League baseball started — where the real excitement lived.

Baseball provided kids their first opportunity to show off for Dad. Now, lying in the hospital bed, Kent could still feel that sweat-stained cap atop his head and the supple smoothness of Dad's linseed-oiled glove on his hand. He was ready, still, to chew on that wad of gum, scratch his crotch, and rack the infield with plastic cleats. Dad would stand proudly watching from behind the chain-link fence.

Kent played baseball through the eighth grade, excelling at pitching, third base, and shortstop, as well as hitting. He threw the only no-hitter in his Little League as a sixth grader. He threw it against the eventual Little League champs. He also drove in the only run. Of course, his steady girlfriend — Juanita Winn — had dumped him that night for another guy, but he eventually charmed her back. He was the first player never to strike out during an entire season.

God granted him speed, and he excelled in track. He also had an early growth spurt, which shaped a physical frame of broad shoulders and long legs — perfect for sports. His speed and size proved ideal for football. And in Texas being the town superjock made you king of the hill with all the trimmings.

Those trimmings were seductive to a growing boy: the cheerleaders, the school beauty queen, preferential treatment by teachers, profiles in the newspaper, college recruiters buying steaks and promising more, little kids wanting autographs, business leaders slapping backs and promising good-paying summer jobs, and finally the dream of signing a major college football scholarship.

Every gradeschool jock wanted to be Mr. Superstar. From an early age, Kent wanted nothing less. And God had given him the body with which to succeed, a body that responded to every command ever given. Until now. So Kent spent the long nights willing his muscles to move.

About a week or so into the restless but therapeutic period, Al unexpectedly returned to Kent's bedside late one night.

"I couldn't sleep," his dad said, pacing the floor. "Thought you might like some company."

The night nurse took a break, leaving them alone. Kent searched his father's sleepy eyes — eyes much like Kent's own. His father's strong jaw and rugged good looks always reminded Kent of Robert Mitchum.

Al had always been so much more than Kent's father. He was the person Kent wanted to golf with, to throw pitches to, to share his confidences. They communicated almost telepathically, understanding one another without words. Kent knew instantly, as his father quit the pacing and pulled up a chair beside the bed, strongly grasping his son's hand, that Al was troubled.

"Son," he began, but his voice broke. He coughed, took a deep breath, and began again, "Son, I feel so helpless," he blurted, but tears again overwhelmed him. "I, I want to do something, but I don't know how to help," he added, burying his head at Kent's side.

Tears streamed down Kent's cheeks as well. Al needed a sign that his only boy was not giving up, that his son still had some fight. The time had come. To this point, Kent's only movement below his shoulders had been a slight bicep curl that could barely raise his supinated hand off the sheets. But he knew his midnight homework owed a dividend.

Okay, Lord, it's me and you, Kent prayed. It's fourth and goal from the thirty. Now's the time we score.

With all his will, Kent concentrated on his right arm. God answered quickly. Kent's flaccid right arm began to rise toward his face. In an uncoordinated and awkward swoop, he raised his arm across his chest. His hand plopped onto his face and he pretended to scratch his nose.

Al's eyes swelled with tears as he wrapped strong arms around Kent and both began sobbing like babies. "I love you, Dad."

"I love you, son," Al said softly. "And whatever it takes, we will beat this thing. Together."

The forcefulness of his father's voice caused Kent to feel as though he could climb Mt. Everest barefooted.

After that night, things started to click. Movement didn't return quickly, but Kent's biceps and wrists became functional. Karen, the physical therapist, started celebrating milestones with poetry:

> Roses are red,
> Violets are blue,
> Kent has a new muscle,
> To help his arm move.
> (It extends the arm —
> can you guess what it's called?)

She had tested a trace of triceps in his right arm, which could mean that his functional level could possibly improve to a C-6 or C-7 in time. Of course, she may as well have spoken Greek, but it did mean he was one muscle closer to being whole again. Damn the triceps, full movement ahead!

And now, two weeks after surgery, Dr. Galbraith had the cervical traction removed. What a relief! No more human telegraph service. No more Frankenstein lookalike! Kent could roll his head from side to side, and he got the semblance of a pillow.

Except for the haircut, Kent looked like himself again. The emergency room scalping had left a nice patch of long hair in the back, which annoyed Al intensely. So, leave it to Dad to fix the style. Al found a local barber to make the house call and complete Kent's Marine Corps burr.

With the traction and most of his hair gone, the family began planning for acute rehabilitation.

You betcha, Kent thought, let's get at it. Put me through three-a-days — I'm ready to walk again. And the first place Mom had mentioned for rehabilitation was Spain.

Not bad. Not bad at all. A little rehab, a little Spanish sun, some Spanish nurses with coal black hair and deep dark tans. We'll give R R a whole new meaning!

The Spain they referred to, however, was a brand new rehabilitation hospital opening right there in Birmingham. Out flew Kent's version of Fantasy Rehab.

But the doctors and his parents decided on another option instead. The Institute for Research and Rehabilitation (T.I.R.R.) in Houston, offered an acute Spinal Cord Injury (SCI) rehab program right in Kent's old backyard — where he had grown up and graduated from high school.

The family started getting excited. Then, on a Sunday evening, the staff attempted to position Kent on a water mattress. Denise helped one of the nurses to turn him.

"Mother," Kent gasped frantically. "Mother! I can't breathe!"

CHAPTER THREE

YOU'LL NEVER WALK AGAIN

Within seconds, the nurses secured an oxygen mask onto Kent's face. "I can't breathe," he mouthed. No words emerged. Helpless. So helpless.

A doctor stethoscoped his chest. A nurse prepared a needle. The doctor stabbed the needle through Kent's skin in search of a vein. He missed. All the while, Kent tried to cough up the mucous filling his lungs.

Six stabs later, the doctor struck blood. From the terse exchanges, Kent gathered that he'd either suffered a stroke, a heart attack, or his lungs had collapsed from pneumonia.

The tests revealed pneumonia, and Kent was rushed to Intensive Care.

In ICU, the doctor blandly said, "This may cause you some discomfort."

Oh, hell — he'd heard that before.

The nightmare became surreal. An oversized plastic tube was shoved through his right nostril, down his throat and into his lungs. It didn't take Jean Dixon to predict that the tube would stay.

The clock ticked. Hours meandered like days, the swell of time slowing to an undulating ripple, then an undertow of reverse. He imagined patterns upon the ceiling or listened to the unbroken buzz of equipment. Again, his family could see him only in short segments. Years lugged by between visits.

He focused on the tube running down his trachea. At regular intervals, the nurses inserted a smaller tube which sucked the fluid from his lungs. In addition, his electrical bed still had to be flipped, turning him face down to the floor. The nurses would unhook his oxygen mask for the thirty to sixty seconds of this process, leaving Kent without air. Unable to talk with the tube inserted and having to hold his

44

breath during the unhooking-turning-rehooking-no-oxygen-procedure, he had no way to communicate. He came close to choking. In the isolation of silence, he alone knew this.

Here they come again, he thought, the flipping procedure at hand. The nurse prepared the bed for the flip. Wait! You haven't fastened the critical joints that prevent me from falling. Wait! I'm gonna land nose first on the floor!

He struggled to move his arms but they were strapped for the transfer. He tried to scream with no oxygen. He contorted his face into Halloween expressions and frantically spoke with his eyes.

Finally the nurse looked at Kent's face. Her own eyes popped open. She wore the look of a scream with no sounds. Seconds before disaster struck, she secured the joints.

Besides the staff's roto-rootering his nasal passage with the water hose, stabbing him with needles, and playing the now-you-can-breathe-now-you-can't game, Kent was left alone. For the first time since his ordeal started, he felt the chill of death.

His resolve wavered as emotional momentum nosedived. After rallying from a 35–0 deficit to tie the score, now, with a second left on the clock, his opponent had maneuvered into position to kick the winning field goal.

Somehow, he had to turn this contest around, get "Big Mo" back on *his* side.

His mind drifted. Back to being the star high school athlete, back to pushing himself beyond his own limits to win even if he sustained injuries in the process. Injuries wiped out most of his junior and senior track seasons. But he still received All-District and All-County honors. One week before the district meet, he reinjured a hamstring. A visit to the sports medicine specialist revealed he actually tore the hamstring from his pelvic girdle. The specialist said Kent had simply pushed beyond his own muscle capacity.

Push through. He had always pushed through. Through the pain. Through the trauma. Winning never meant nearly as much as it did now, but he'd always played his best, always given 100 percent, then dug down to give a little more.

For five days in ICU, Kent hovered precariously close to death. Though no one said this to him, he knew. He knew as he heard the hum of the machines that sustained his life. He knew as he suffocated, lungs sputtering with each breath. He knew through his loneliness and fear. It was so cold here, so very cold.

But he knew, more than anything else, that he was not yet ready to leave. Sports had taught him to never give in. To never give up. His playing field was different now, the stakes higher, and his resources less certain. If he were to die, the pneumonia would have to beat him. He would not surrender.

"Well, you're chipper this morning," the nurse said, smiling as she sought even more blood.

Kent smiled back at her. You would be too, he thought, if they finally removed a water hose from your nose. Or maybe it was the recovery from pneumonia and everyone returning to the planning mode. "Yeah," he answered. "This little vacation at your spa has been a real relaxing experience. But I think I'll try Club Med next time. I hear they actually let you leave with the blood you brought."

She laughed as she finished and left. His mother came in with yet more well-wishers' cards. A stylish pantsuit adorned her trim figure and a smile spread across her face, emphasizing her strong jawline. She almost looked like her normal self. Kent grinned.

"Governor Wallace called," Denise said, shaking flipped, dark hair over one shoulder. "He's flying us to Houston on his plane. The hospital has asked that we leave early to keep down the media circus."

Kent frowned. "I hate to just sneak out," he replied.

Denise nodded and sighed. "So do I. Especially since the people of Alabama have been so wonderful. But it's probably best, Kent. It's the least we can do for the hospital."

This was true, he thought. The hospital had coped with all the calls and letters from folks around the country. Alabamans especially had been helpful and kind. Not just Governor Wallace and Bear Bryant, but regular folks as well. A dentist his parents met through the ordeal, Dr. Sanderson, came and cleaned Kent's teeth. A small thing, but it sure made him feel good. And other new friends, Harold and Joni Blach, had special glasses made so Kent could see television from his awkward position. The Alabama Alumni Association picked up

46

the motel bill. And now Governor Wallace provided for his trip to Houston.

A thought tripped across Kent's mind about where TCU fit into all this, but surely they were helping.

And now, *nally,* off to rehabilitation and getting back on his feet. He would be walking in no time.

His mom started reading cards, but he hardly heard. He noticed how drawn she had become, knowing this was why she didn't look exactly like her normal fiery self. Mom had her own setback while he was in ICU. One morning she rounded the corner to find his room empty. No Kent. Not even the bed. She sank to the floor. Though nurses rushed in with reassurances that all was okay, his mom remained a walking corpse for days. Only now had she begun to recover, though she would never admit any of it to him. God, if only I could keep my folks from seeing me like this! Well, that's why we're going to Houston: for full recovery.

So on November 26, 1974, a month after the accident, the Waldreps boarded a plane bound for the future. Kent traveled on a stretcher, accompanied by his mom, dad, older sister, Carole, and a doctor and nurse. Most of the way, he slept.

An ambulance and a car from T.I.R.R. met them at Hobby Airport in Houston. Twenty-five minutes later, they arrived at the center.

Though they left Alabama at 5:00 a.m. to avoid press and well-wishers, none greeted them at T.I.R.R. No one but medical staffers and white-coats. Good, Kent thought. We don't want to cause more inconvenience.

They rolled him down several halls to Station B. Six other spinal cord injuries and one empty bed next to the door filled this cell.

The room spoke of doom. Gray, dull walls faced him, no pictures, no color. Nothing cheery. And with seven people occupying the space of a normal office, privacy would be nonexistent.

At the end of the room, a sliding glass door offered a speck of life, opening to the outside, opening to the walking world.

The other patients stared at him, little light in their eyes. And my God, they looked like characters in a scene from Auschwitz — skinny to the point of starvation, hollow-eyed and drawn. The room smelled of urine and felt of death.

"Hello, Kent," a doctor said, stopping at Kent's bunk. "I'm Dr. Carter. I'll be your physician while you're with us. The rest of your team will arrive shortly." Dr. Carter spoke in a monotone as he scanned Kent's chart, resting the metal clipboard on his paunchy belly. He stared through thick, black-framed glasses and then abruptly turned and left.

Kent's folks had gone to fill out paperwork. He scanned the room. In no time in sauntered another white-coat.

"Good morning!" the skinny young man said cheerfully, pulling up a chair and sitting next to the bunk. "I'll be your social therapist."

Social therapist? Kent wondered, saying hello.

"We've heard a lot about you! In fact, the media is giving us quite a fit as we try to keep them away. How do you feel about talking with them?"

Kent answered, "I have no problem with the press. They've all been really nice."

"Good. We'll arrange a meeting once you've adjusted," the therapist quipped.

"Adjusted?"

"You know, once the reality of being paralyzed and confined to a wheelchair the rest of your life sinks in."

Kent jolted. Huh?

"What reality?"

"Mr. Waldrep," he began, with a swish through the air of one slender hand, "you've been an athlete most of your life. My job is to now teach you to come to grips with your new reality — living in a wheelchair *for the rest of your life.*

The muscles in Kent's neck tightened. His teeth clenched. This bastard, like he can pass judgment over *my* life! Who the hell was he? That Kent couldn't slam a right hook into the jerk's pointy nose made him madder.

"Get the hell out of my sight you dirty son-of-a-bitch!"

The shrink scurried from the room.

Kent looked around, but the rest of the patients seemed oblivious.

With the exception of one about Kent's age, they stared at the walls or slept.

The young man turned to Kent. "He's a prince, that resident shrink of ours."

The guy's head sported a fashionable burr, just like Kent's own. But he must have had problems with his medieval halo traction because deep indentions notched his forehead and temples. He could star in a horror movie.

"Welcome to rehab from hell. I'm Charles."

About then entered a bevy of rehabilitation specialists, one after another. His new nurse and all the therapists — physical, occupational, respiratory (at least the social one had been banished) — plus the urologist and dietician. If Kent could have felt his stomach, he knew a heavy lead weight would be sinking into its pit. What the hell had they gotten into?

"They're making jokes behind your back," Katie whispered to Denise in the hallway. Katie was leaving after having spent the weekend — as she had since they had arrived in Houston. She came on Friday evenings and left Sunday afternoons. For Kent's emotional well-being, this woman had proved a godsend. "Kent hears them."

"They can just laugh," Denise said, hazel eyes flashing. "Like I care what these idiots think. Maybe they'll bust a girdle."

Katie grasped her hand. "He'd never make it here without you."

Denise sighed. "Well, I don't know about that. Though he sure might starve to death."

Al had already returned home to work, Terry Lynn to school, Carole to her family. Katie was the last to go. Kent's care was left to Denise through the week.

"How the others make it without family is beyond me," Katie added, her fragile face drooping somewhat as she glanced back at the room.

"Kent's got all of us," Denise answered, squeezing her hand. They hugged, and Katie, too, left for the normal world.

Denise stood a while longer in the hall before leaving for her apartment. The orderlies were making fun of the patients again, and she put her hands over her ears. They always made fun of the patients, and most especially of Kent since his mother stuck around and caused trouble.

Actually, she made sure he was fed and asked questions about his progress and therapy. All patients' treatment came from a cookie cutter mold — no individualization here. And she *did* do much of the staff's work, the cleaning and care that they couldn't seem to give the spinal cord patients under their supervision. These people could curse her for doing their jobs until the roof caved in.

The entire area smelled of urine and other bodily functions. With eight beds separated at times only by curtains, privacy eluded them. All the patients used the bathroom at the same time, and the smells would almost do you in. Some patients had left since Kent's arrival, but most looked and acted like living death. There seemed to be no souls left in their decimated bodies.

None coped well emotionally. None had family to help, and only some had visitors. Charles Fox's family came, and he and Kent seemed to be doing the best, psychologically speaking. Charles gave the nurses holy hell whenever possible. Denise and Kent liked him a lot. The handling of patients left much to be desired. The care given each person correlated directly with how much the aides liked him or her. No one offered hope of *ever* walking again. Any remaining shred of dignity patients possessed was systematically stripped, day by day, until most lost the will to try. To the doctors and staff, hope was a four-letter word.

Denise persisted in her questions. Wasn't someone, someplace, any place researching the possibilities of a cure? No. There is no hope, she was told over and over again. All professionals gave her the textbook response, "The spinal cord does not regenerate; therefore all paralysis present three to six months post-injury will be permanent." There was no need for research. None was being conducted.

She just couldn't believe it.

Driving to her apartment, Denise Waldrep pondered this. Their experience in Alabama had been so very different. Of course, no one used the term "paralysis," at least not until late into the stay. The ignorance was truly bliss. But now she wanted answers, and it seemed no one else had even asked the questions. How could that be?

And the difference in attitude! The staff in Alabama cared, fostered hope, acted like human beings. The instant the family arrived

50

at T.I.R.R., Denise sensed all this would change. The place portrayed an eerie gloom. Once a polio ward, it merely evolved into another lifeless cell.

Other than the time in Alabama when the nurses almost dropped Kent while flipping the bed, his care was exemplary. Oh, there was that day she trucked into ICU to find his room empty. ICU had already lost one patient that morning. The nurses searched for Denise to relay the message that they had moved him, but she found the room first. It was the only time she allowed herself to *feel* that the family might lose their boy. Never again, she vowed. Never again would she allow that sentiment.

Now, if they could just make it through this mess. Denise knew the staff hated her for making their jobs easier — and for questioning. Always questioning. She and Al sent the social therapist packing the first day after she gave him a good dose of her temper. Later, she found that Kent had done the same. Though the medical community might be defeatist, the Waldreps were not without hope.

They learned a lot this month. Learned which foods to eat and which to avoid, though culinary successes never emerged from the hospital commissary. Buzzards circled that place.

Kent went through preparations for the transition from lying on his back to sitting. After being prone for so long, his blood pressure nose dived as his head was raised higher than his pillow. Finally, though, they had him sitting up.

And of course they learned to prevent pressure sores — the nemesis of all paraplegics and quadriplegics. Lying in one place for too long caused an open sore the patient could not feel, and it could take forever to heal.

Denise mastered the catheterization process. Sterility proved the main consideration. Kent had not contracted one bladder infection while in Alabama — yet another testament to that hospital and staff's adeptness. The regime began with recatheterization every three hours. Fluid intake and urine extract corresponded directly. In a regular progression, fluid intake increased, and the procedure was reduced to every four, then six, then eight hours.

Kent constantly complained that his fluid intake was too restricted, and he needed to drink more to kick off his bladder. Denise suspected

51

her son was correct. Well, there would be time to test the theory. Right now, learning the basics and bolstering his spirits were the primary goals, though Kent's fortitude never flagged. He inspired the whole family. But thank God for Terry Lynn and Carole and Katie and Al.

Bless Al's heart. After being so practical during the initial crisis — when Denise herself was so foggy — he had difficulty dealing with the rehabilitation process. The reality of his son's condition hit him at T.I.R.R.

Basically, she and Al's roles reversed. He cried a lot. But their son never knew this. Al would go through his grieving and return to being the stoic father. In the meantime, Denise and Kent made light of things, and lived one day at a time.

"Oh, man," Charles Fox said, "here comes Marla." Kent glanced quickly over. Sure enough, their favorite nurse floated in on long, shapely legs. With her dark hair swept up, she looked like an angel. Well, maybe a fallen angel.

"Hey, baby," Charles said, "we're having a session tonight."

"You guys," Marla responded laughing.

Charles winked at her and said, "You gotta come." The "sessions" he spoke of were "Coffee, Tea, or Sex Sessions" that the inmates hosted once a week. Basically, these consisted of viewing dirty films, and Marla was everybody's choice to participate in the watching. Everyone tried to impress her, even the vague and almost comatose patients Kent hardly knew.

Of course, this proved a double-edged sword. Since all the nurses tended to all the patients' plumbing, they saw everybody naked. You got used to it pretty quickly. This didn't bother you so much when the nurse was old or frumpy or otherwise undesirable. But when, like Marla, she was beautiful and young, well....

"Hey, you got a banana under the sheets or you just glad to see me?" Marla asked Charles.

Spinal cord patients are prone to reflexive erections, and Charles sported one now.

"Goddamnit," he muttered.

Had it been anybody but Marla, Kent knew Charles wouldn't have

52

cared, would have probably made a dirty joke. But with Marla. . . . Kent knew the feeling. That you actually couldn't feel the sensation didn't alleviate the embarrassment.

"I just don't get it," Kent began with a grin. "The one body part that will move we can't control."

Charles laughed and Marla did too. She said, "So goes life," before moving on to the others.

Charles looked to Kent and said, "Merry Christmas."

"Yeah," Kent replied. He stared around the dismal room, at decorations consisting of a few red bows and a very anemic scotch pine. I gotta make it Christmas, he thought. But how?

Ah, Katie.

Katie hung in there the first month in Alabama and still did as they both adjusted to the reality of T.I.R.R. She visited every weekend, and they talked constantly by phone through the week. The visits were hard on her, though she didn't complain. But Kent could see it in her eyes, see her flinch sometimes when she didn't know he saw, see her avert her gaze from the others, their disabilities so overwhelming.

In addition to patients with spinal cord injuries, patients with head injuries and muscular dystrophy as well as ventilator-dependent patients and amputees filled the ward. Kent struggled with getting used to the myriad of miseries too, and he lived here full time. Topping off this depressing environment, the staff's negative attitudes could crush anyone's spirit. But not Katie's. Her eyes still sparkled when she saw him, and her grin lit up the entire room.

Katie insulated Kent from the suffering and tragedy surrounding them. She protected him from all those labels, the awful words. Paralysis. Paraplegia. Medical science called Kent a quadriplegic — suffering paralysis in both legs and arms. The term made him feel like an outcast in a leper colony. As S ren Kierkegaard said, "When you label me, you negate me."

Katie helped him to feel human again. She provided a window to Kent's past that the injury was quietly stealing — a past he desperately wanted back. Kent felt certain her courage would ride out this misfortune with him.

They spoke of marriage, of a wedding to take place as soon as he completed rehabilitation and could walk down the aisle. That she still loved him and stayed committed to him made life bearable. It made him feel wanted.

A ring, he thought, a ring would be the perfect Christmas gift. Not an engagement ring exactly, more of a promise ring, a get-through-rehab-and-back-to-real-life ring. Yeah.

As Christmas approached, Katie came again to visit. Shyly, Kent brought forth his tiny package.

Katie immediately began crying. "It's so beautiful," she said softly. She hugged and kissed him and proceeded to show every employee and patient her ring.

But she traveled back home for Christmas day. And though most of Kent's family came, this Christmas seemed something akin to a vacation at Alcatraz. So how to bring in the New Year?

"Hey, Kent," Charles began one morning, "we need to have us a New Year's Eve party."

"Now that oughta be easy to plan," Kent replied. "Should we send out invitations or just phone all our friends?"

Charles shook his indented head. He and Kent clowned around a lot, yelling, throwing the building blocks from OT. You could always expect the unexpected from Charles.

"I betcha we can do it," he continued. "We just gotta keep it secret."

Kent rubbed his chin. "And keep all the Nurse Ratcheds away."

"You got it."

So they planned. Kent bribed a couple of male nursing attendants to buy the champagne and smuggle in some award-winning films. Okay, so those movies were not the kind kids could see, but hey, none of them were kids here, right?

Charles made certain none of the other patients would know until the very last minute. Secrecy was imperative for success.

Forty-eight hours in advance, they had organized champagne, films, and other assorted delicacies (namely, a select group of nurses and therapists who qualified on their beauty scale). Several physical therapists and the two voluptuous respiratory therapists planned to cart the lucky patients to a secret hideaway. Due to catheterization schedules and routine patient rounds, the celebration had to be scheduled for 9:00 p.m. It would climax (hopefully) some forty-five minutes later.

54

As New Year's Eve day progressed, Charles and Kent couldn't look at one another without cracking up.

"We're two clever cripples, man," Kent told him.

"You bet your ass we are."

They went to dinner, unable to keep from grinning, knowing the other patients would enjoy this party as much as they. Finishing dinner, they began inching back down the hall and to the ward.

In the nurse's station, two ragged nurses talked. One wore a size forty uniform, and the other looked somewhat shriveled, her hair in a severe bun.

"He should be fired," the bunned one said.

"At the very least," the obese one agreed.

Charles and Kent froze.

The bunned one continued, "Carrying all those bottles of champagne. And on a paralysis ward. Hmph."

"Procedure," the other huffed. "We must always follow procedure."

"Goddamnit," Charles muttered under his breath.

"They got caught," Kent said, more in disbelief than deduction. They got caught, he repeated to himself. No.

Slowly they finished the trek to the ward, much slower than usual, the week-long grins ripped from their faces. More than the celebration left their hearts. In silence, they both stared at the stark ceiling.

Late, late that night, Kent felt someone shaking his arm. He and Charles both awakened with a start. The two voluptuous RTs — the heavy-breathing ladies — sat at their bedsides, toting flasks of champagne.

Through muffled laughter and toasting cheer, they rung in the New Year.

Whatever you are doing as the new year dawns, or so the saying goes, you will be doing the whole year through. Beating the rehab system, Kent thought, snuggling into his pillow. I can do that. If I never do another thing, I *will* beat this system. And one day I'll change it, see if I won't, he said, submitting to slumber.

55

The new year began with the promise of his first weekend pass. This not only set a much needed goal, but signaled the homestretch of acute rehab. Home smiled from the horizon.

The weekend of January 26–27 marked the dates for that first pass. As a prelude to it, Dr. Carter gave approval for Kent to attend the TCU-Rice basketball game. TCU Sports Information Director Jim Garner and some friends would help Kent's mother with the ten-minute trek.

Sitting at the end of the TCU bench, Kent fidgeted awkwardly. He didn't know the basketball players. They all seemed so big, so strong, so agile.

Though he had gained a fair measure of confidence in his appearance, he soon realized this was because his fellow inmates at T.I.R.R. looked as if they were cast for a hunger relief film. Here in this gym among healthy ball players, he felt lost. His muscles had atrophied and his once wash-board stomach flopped. For his first time ever, he didn't belong around other athletes. Wishing desperately to disappear, Kent sat and cheered for TCU.

The next day, his drawn face and scrubby burr haircut made the AP and UPI wires. Throughout America, this gaunt photo graced the front pages as he shouted for TCU to beat Rice.

He returned to his typical schedule — up at 5:30 a.m. Fight with the nurses about how they dressed him. Breakfast. Then his mom bathed his upper body. One and a half hours of physical therapy. An hour of occupational therapy. Lunch. Nothing to do until late afternoon weight lifting. At 5:30 p.m., supper.

Sometimes in the afternoons, classes were given on nutrition, skin care, health care, or bladder and bowel function. On alternate Thursdays, sex therapy classes were held, consisting mainly of grainy, awfully acted porno films. These sex classes proved worse than useless. Each was a bad joke.

And everyone had too much free time.

Now, though, he was prepared for his weekend with Katie. He could tolerate sitting up for eight hour stretches. His catheterization was down to every six hours. He mastered wearing his contact lenses again. The process of inserting each tiny disk with limp fingers amazed the nursing staff. Both he and his mom were as gratified by the staff's shock as by the event. You ain't seen nothing yet, he thought as they ooed and ahhed at his dexterity.

Saturday morning they traveled to Denise's rented apartment, not far from T.I.R.R. Not far, Kent thought, but worlds and lifetimes away. A real place, with Katie and substances to eat that resembled food along with the beverage of his choice.

He also planned to test his own bladder theory. All along he argued that his fluids were too restricted, that he needed to drink more. He postulated that the "tastes great, less feeling" variety might stimulate a bladder awakening. As usual, the staff ignored him. Well, he'd just see.

They sat on the couch all day, watching television. Kent consumed his first post-injury beer — grains processed the way God intended. Katie laughed as he grinned and licked the foam from his lips.

Charles Fox and his family stopped by and Denise cooked chicken fried steaks with gravy and mashed potatoes and salad.

"I have died and gone to heaven," Kent said, sopping up the last of the gravy.

"The Nurse Ratcheds would bust their guts, they see us eating all this."

Both grinned and drank another beer. A hundred years had passed since Kent enjoyed an afternoon this much.

By evening and after drinking four beers, he felt ready for a little romance. Nervous, but ready. Denise changed him into pajamas and folded out the couch into a king-sized bed. Then she retired to her room until time for the next catheterization, about four hours away.

Kent lay quietly on the couch, Katie softly stroking his forehead. He tried to quell the nervousness. Though the paralysis did have its effects, it didn't quell his attraction for the ladies. Lying next to Katie aroused every sexual instinct he had ever known. But what would happen? Had all the plumbing been knocked out? Feelings, intense as lightning bolts, arose. Katie sensed it, kissing him.

Her kisses were long and soft, sweet. But Kent knew, for all his once-assured confidence, his boldness with girls had been somewhat squelched. Unless Katie initiated the advances, he was content to hold her close. So they hugged and kissed.

"After you finish school and I finish too," Katie said as they spoke of marriage.

"And after I fully recover," Kent added. "I plan to *walk* down the aisle."

"We'll have three kids."

Kent nodded. "And I'll turn to professional golf."

Katie cocked her head, flashing that grin, and said, "My husband, the professional golfer. You'll have to wear those silly clothes."

"And the ugly jackets that when you win all of a sudden don't look so ugly," he added.

Life was going to be really good.

Denise's appearance with the catheterization kit brought them back to earth. Since Katie had never watched the procedure, she stepped into the other room.

Just before Denise started to insert the catheter tube, Kent's comatose bladder erupted, sending up a bright yellow stream onto Denise's robe.

She jumped back, grinning. "Did you see that?"

"Yeah, what did you do, not insert the catheter fully?"

"Lord, no!" she exclaimed. "You did that before I even got ready."

Kent inhaled deeply, a grin spreading over his face.

"You mean I pissed on my own?"

"And you're starting again!"

Kent slapped the couch. "I *told* you those beers would do the trick. Just wait till Dr. Carter hears about this — he'll probably piss in his own pants."

Both laughing, Denise finished the procedure to make sure the bladder had fully emptied. She got very little residue.

"This is January 26th," Kent said.

"Exactly three months after the injury," Denise finished the thought.

For a few moments, Kent looked into her eyes — eyes filled with what neither would speak. As his mom left again, Kent knew their hope had not been futile.

Throughout the night, Kent and Katie talked of this small victory, of how his body had responded, of God's healing powers. Then they slept till noon.

Sunday they watched golf and Al brought take-out fried chicken, and everyone tried to ignore Kent's quickly approaching deadline. But it came anyway. Back to the dungeon.

And back to therapy, which seemed so infantile. Though the free weekend marked the start of Kent's last thirty days at T.I.R.R., his frustration mounted. His physical therapist, though sweet and caring, was no Vince Lombardi. Occupational therapy had consisted of constructing building blocks. His therapist coached him into using a wrist and hand prosthesis, which had been fitted for him early on.

One day, while Kent was constructing block castles, several TCU coaches — Shof and Jimmy Thomas (the backfield coach), David McGinnis and Royce Huffman (graduate assistants involved in recruiting Kent to TCU) — came for a visit. Many had come regularly, and Kent always looked forward to seeing them. His teammates, however, couldn't cope with his injury. Some visited once, not to return. Most stayed away.

Kent was testing his hand and wrist devices when the coaches arrived.

"Kent," Mrs. Parker, the OT, said, "why don't you demonstrate your new skills with a building block exhibition?"

Kent resisted. If he couldn't wiggle a toe or lift a leg, why put on a show? This was bullshit.

"Come on now," she continued, "let's show them your progress."

To her continued encouragement, Kent began stacking. He clumsily put one block upon another. Without looking at the pitying gazes of his coaches, he choked back tears of humiliation and continued. Nineteen blocks. An OT record. What a big boy!

As everyone cheered, Kent tried to evaporate.

The device felt robotic, and right away he became obsessed with ridding himself of it. So, to supplement the building blocks and improve dexterity, he played cards with his mom. Gin rummy mostly. And dominoes, too. This extracurricular activity shocked the nurses; the staff always scoffed at anything beyond standard procedure.

And Dr. Carter, who never managed more than a somewhat bored grunt to Kent's initiatives, made fewer and fewer appearances. The whole medical team reminded Kent of inept coaches that he had played for.

When Kent was a sophomore, his parents moved the family to Alvin. The move itself didn't crush him, but the transfer to Kent's athletic archrival school did. The University Scholastic League rule in

59

Texas prohibiting towns from enticing good athletes by offering jobs to their parents forced Kent out of varsity ball for a year. Patience did not come easily to a fifteen-year-old football star. But he learned.

He responded by blasting through junior varsity, finishing the season leading the district in rushing (while playing quarterback three-fourths of the time), scoring nineteen touchdowns rushing and five touchdowns passing, and kicking two field goals plus seventeen extra points. In one game, he carried the ball five times for five touchdowns and gained 235 yards. In the same game, he threw for another touchdown, threw for a two-point conversion, and kicked four extra points. Varsity football here I come, he thought.

The school was elevated to 4A status, and the successful varsity head coach departed all in one whack. Just another setback. But the new coach, Harden Cooper, would be to Kent what Delilah was to Samson, what Nixon was to the presidency, what the Super Bowl would become to the Buffalo Bills.

In two seasons Coach Cooper would attempt to reverse what God and hard work had finely tuned and conditioned over sixteen years. He would try to "teach" Kent to run with the ball. He completely wasted Kent's natural abilities. Instead, Cooper used Kent as a halfback in a T-bone attack — an offense needing a big, strong offensive line and a quick-footed quarterback. Alvin had neither.

Those final two years of high school football provided a study in self-determination and survival. The players lacked confidence in the coaching. The coaches, frustrated by lopsided losses, took it out on the team.

Kent learned then, and saw reinforced around him now, that coaches had to recognize and relate to God-given talent. Communication and interaction between players and coaches shaped winners. Was that such a difficult concept?

Despite playing for a team that won only four games in his last two years, Kent still attracted scholarship offers from twenty-five colleges. Strictly football offers comprised the majority, but some combined football with track or golf. Offers ranged from Walla Walla College in Washington to Nebraska to the Naval Academy. He even underwent a complete military physical for the Navy, but decided his stomach couldn't withstand seven years at sea.

Above all, Kent learned some valuable lessons — lessons that now proved vital in a way he could never have foreseen. He learned to wait out the bad times and focus on what lay ahead. He learned to trust his own instincts and judgment, to rely on Kent. And he learned to never, *ever* believe when someone said, "You are not able to do that," in reference to his own body.

All things happen for a reason, he thought, lying in his bunk. God does not provide growth opportunities for the heck of it. This place could preach forever that he would never walk again. Kent Waldrep would show them that be could. They could point to the textbook definition that "the spinal cord does not regenerate; therefore all paralysis present three to six months post-injury will be permanent," all they wanted. He would prove the textbooks wrong.

If no research for a cure was being performed, Kent would find out why.

As D-Day for discharge grew closer, the preparations for care were made, and equipment was bought, including a custom-fitted wheelchair, Kent and Denise became more optimistic. This state seemed a bit odd after the negative T.I.R.R. experience, but they understood now that the progress Kent made would be on his own, with the help of his family.

During that last month, Kent spent every weekend at the apartment with Katie and his family and friends. Lots of folks visited and this boosted his morale even more. He and Katie spent the nights discussing their future, holding one another, and kissing as they spoke of finishing school, getting married, and their strong faith in God.

Right before his release, Katie and Kent talked late into the night.

Katie sat next to him, biting a fingernail.

"Kent," she began, "is it okay with you if I go with a date to the sorority dance?"

The bottom dropped out from under him. "What?"

Katie stared at her hands.

"You want my okay to go on a date?"

"Yeah," she said and paused. Then added quickly, "You know it wouldn't mean anything."

Kent shook. Not mean anything? Katie? My girlfriend, my love? Where are you going?

61

"What, um, what even brought this idea up?" he asked finally. "I've encouraged you to go out with friends, to parties, but you haven't gone. You haven't complained."

"I know," she replied, voice stronger now. "But I miss, well, I'd just be going with Jeff, so I knew you'd understand."

Kent's jaw clenched and his blood boiled. "You mean Jeff asked you out or you asked him?"

"It was sort of mutual," she answered meekly. Great, just great. She's going out with a little dipshit defensive back who I used to routinely run over, through, or anything else I wanted. And he's not nearly as cute as me!

uietly, he said, "Damn, Katie."

Tears welled in her brown eyes and spilled down her cheeks.

"Don't cry," Kent said, his own eyes filling. For a while in the darkness, they held one another and wept.

In the end he consented. Katie vowed never-ending love. But he knew, as she slept softly beside him and he stared at the ceiling, that the end was near.

The next week, with hope and optimism undimmed, Kent and his family left T.I.R.R. for good. He left the gloom of gray walls, the hopeless prognosis. His future spread uncertainly before him. One day at a time, as his mom kept saying. They would plan one day at a time. In his head, he knew there would be no Katie to lean on, though his heart couldn't yet accept that.

Whatever may come, Kent would rely on the strength of his mom, dad, sisters, and God. And he would rely on the strength within himself.

Kent, in his sophomore year at TCU, wasn't happy watching from the sidelines.

Photo taken by Kent's grandfather, Jack Sauer, after the TCU/Texas A&M game, one week before the Alabama game in October, 1974.

Kent on the stretcher near the Alabama bench after his paralyzing injury. TCU's team doctor, Dr. Etier, is behind the sunglasses. That's nurse Barbara McClary at Kent's side. No. 62 is TCU tackle Merle Wang.

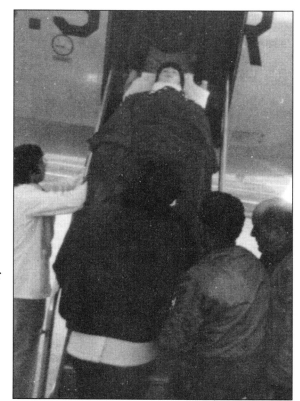

Kent being loaded into an Air Force plane provided by Governor Wallace for the trip to Houston and T.I.R.R. on November 26, 1974.

Kent at home in Grand Prairie in March, 1975 shortly after his release from T.I.R.R. The orthotic prosthesis on his right hand helps him to feed himself.

Kent, with TCU teammates, at the 1975 Football Awards Banquet where he won the Ralph Lowe Award for Sportsmanship.

Legendary Alabama Coach Paul "Bear" Bryant greets Kent on his return to Legion Field in October of 1975, one year after the injury.

Paramedic Barbara McClary was Kent's "angel" who never left his side during the first few hours following the injury. Barbara and her family would become lifelong friends. This picture was taken during Kent's return to Birmingham in October of 1975.

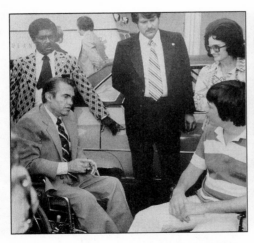 

LEFT: Alabama Governor and 1975 presidential candidate George Wallace visited with Kent during a campaign swing through Dallas/Fort Worth in 1976. Aways supportive, Governor Wallace remained in constant touch with the family during the early years.

RIGHT: Former TCU Sports Information Director Jim Garner made sure Kent had a reserved spot in the TCU press box. In the late 1970s Jim hired Kent as his assistant and public address announcer for home football and basketball games. In the mid-1980s TCU replaced Kent's seating in the press box with a Coke machine.

LEFT: NFL Hall of Famer Roger Staubach was an early supporter of Kent's and a source of inspiration. Roger and Kent are shown here in 1976 at a Texas Hall of Fame function.

RIGHT: Kent in the walker at Polenov Institute.

 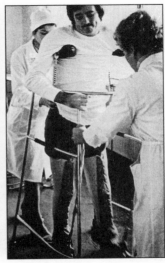

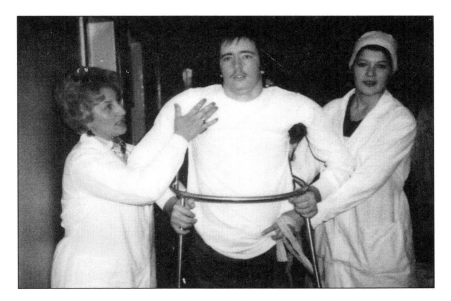

"Walking" was a big part of the physical therapy in Leningrad. Helen (left) and Olga (right) marched Kent up and down the halls daily while other patients cheered.

LEFT: Part of the Russian team of doctors at Polenov Neurosurgical Institute, where Kent spent three months in the fall of 1978. Nona, the interpreter provided by the U.S. Consulate, is at center, behind Kent.

RIGHT: Leningrad wasn't all hard work and bad food. Kent managed to win the attention of a lovely Russian girl, Alla. She was a heart patient who taught Kent Russian as she practiced her English while listening to Kent's music cassettes.

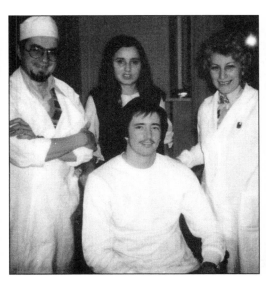

Al, Denise, and Kent
in front of the Polenov
Institute in Leningrad.

Kent's father, Al, gives him enzyme injections at home in Texas.

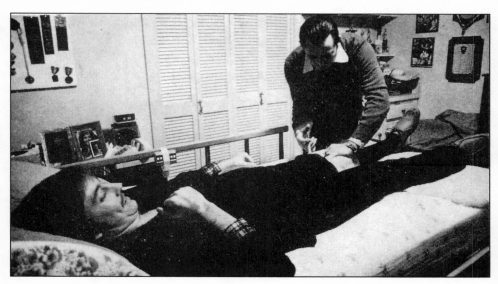

Part Two

Freedom is what you do with what's been done to you.

— Jean Paul Sartre

✧ CHAPTER FOUR ✧

CLIMBING BACK

On February 26, 1975, exactly three months after arriving at T.I.R.R., Kent and Denise flew home to Grand Prairie, Texas. Al packed and closed the apartment and then drove to their new home as well. Neither Kent nor Denise had seen it.

No press covered the departure. No one from TCU came, nor offered any aid.

At Dallas–Forth Worth International Airport, only Katie, accompanied by a girlfriend and a dozen or so family friends, met the plane. No press. And not one person from TCU.

As Kent was transferred into the car, his catheter leaked. Great timing, he muttered.

They arrived at the new house to a combined homecoming/ housewarming party put on by close friends. Martha Wright, long-time family friend, decorated, cooked, and organized the lavish celebration. Amid the food and fanfare, Kent and Denise hurried to find his new bedroom and change his pants.

When they emerged, Kent noticed once more that neither TCU teammates nor coaches came. Playing for a team, any team, forms close emotional ties. Along with the other sensations Kent lost last October, his teammates' camaraderie appeared severed as well.

Oh, his legs had some sensation, but not much — a tingling, like when hitting your funny bone. The prickling was always intense. Even his arms tingled most of the way down. And still he wore his corset. In front of Katie, the family, and friends, embarrassment over his appearance grew.

Kent hadn't been home for an hour when Katie kissed his forehead and said, "I gotta go."

"Do you have to?" he asked.

She nodded, looking past him, then smiled, thanked Denise, and left. For a time Kent watched her fading image. Then he returned to the party.

Through those first weeks, few visitors came. Not one teammate stopped by except offensive lineman Jim Blackwelder, who, along with his girlfriend, taught Kent to play chess. Al and Denise's friends, however, visited often. He did receive letters from some of the Birmingham hospital staff, and especially from Karen, his Alabama physical therapist. And from Governor Wallace and Coach Bryant. Of course, the press kept up with everything.

The catheter continued to leak. And though the new home was nice, and the family friends good company, Kent sorely missed his friends. He was lonely — an emotion he never counted on coming home to. And Katie, ah, Katie.

Time lengthened between her visits. Katie was dating again. One afternoon, his ex-girlfriend Lori and some of her sorority sisters came to call.

Since his catheter kept leaking, Kent started covering his legs with a blanket. When Lori entered the room, he was sitting in his wheelchair, blanket draped across his lap, looking every bit the TV cripple. And he knew it.

"Hey, hotshot," Lori said. She halted a few feet from him as if stopped by a steel curtain.

Kent swallowed. Lori was so pretty — petite, dark, black hair cascading past her waist. But her brown eyes wouldn't look into his and the lump expanded in Kent's throat. He'd never quite gotten over Lori, and for her to see him like this.

Lori fidgeted. Her pouty lips turned downward though she tried hard to smile. But she couldn't. She talked of school, of some trip over spring break, her gaze darting around the room. She never spoke of Kent. Within ten minutes she trudged to the kitchen to talk with Denise while her friends awkwardly kept Kent company. In the background, he heard the soft sounds of Lori crying.

Weeks passed. Visitors dwindled. Katie ceased coming at all. A song kept dancing through Kent's mind, a country ballad popular in recent years about a girl named Kathy leaving her man. The names transposed themselves as the lyrics played over and over on the haunting melody:

66

I lie here and stare, wondering why?
You vanished without a single
Goodbye.
Why did you leave me here all alone?
Can't you see I still breathe, and I'm still
flesh and bone?

Damn, Katie, why now?
The halls of my memory they echo
So loud — saying
Damn, Katie, why now?

Do you not think I'm the man I used to be?
Or is it you can't face
Reality?
I've been hit by missiles, went head-on with trains
But nothing has ever caused so
Much pain.

Damn, Katie, why now?
The halls of my memory they echo
So loud — saying
Damn, Katie, why now?

You just faded away like dust in the sun
Like a wisp of smoke you were
Gone.
I guess we all know the real reason why.
If I weren't so angry I think I would
Cry.

Kent battled one bladder infection after another. Each took ten or so days to bounce back from. Bladder and kidney infections pose some of the toughest complications every patient with a spinal cord injury has to confront. Catheterization only irritates the problem. Research into treatment seemed nonexistent, and urologists merely hit-and-missed at the situation with antibiotics. The stress started telling on Kent. His appearance deteriorated.

On the morning of the annual TCU football banquet and awards dinner, yet another infection took hold. Kent's temperature shot to

$103°$. But he was going to the banquet, and he'd be damned if anyone would know of the infection.

Al, Denise, Terry Lynn, and Kent drove to TCU, for Kent to accept the Rob Lowe Sportsmanship Award from the Frog Club. The fever's chills racked his body. But he swore his family to silence. He didn't want pity from teammates and coaches; he'd felt enough pity, thank you, to last the rest of his life. He didn't want to hear, "Oh, Kent, you're sick and shouldn't be here," or, "It's so great of you to come, in your condition."

That wasn't why he was here.

He came because it meant everything to be around his teammates. The award was sort of secondary. Perhaps by breaking the ice this way, more of his friends would feel comfortable about stopping by the house to visit. God, how he missed them.

Kent stared out the window, stared at anything rather than himself. The infections had halted his physical progress and caused him to lose more weight. His gaunt face reflected from the automobile's glass. Clothes hung on his body, the smaller sized pants hitting shins, about six inches too short.

How would his teammates respond? He hadn't been around them since the accident. Looking as he did made being out in public uncomfortable. To be on display was awful. Remembering his first outing from T.I.R.R. to the TCU-Rice basketball game, Kent shivered.

In the banquet hall, the energy from his teammates and coaches cloaked him. But there was something else in the players' eyes. They all had it, an expression that was not of pity or disdain. It was a faint look of fear.

How difficult it must have been for each of them to play football after his injury, to harbor that haunting feeling that at any second, on any play....

Kent considered what he would say. He had pondered for weeks. He made no notes, and when he began to speak, the words flowed from his heart.

"I'm very moved and touched by this special honor you're giving me," Kent began, his voice strong. "If there's anything a TCU football player would have learned in the past two years, it's certainly sportsmanship." Through laughter in the banquet room, Kent paused. The team had not exactly been in the running for a national title. "Losing the games we did, we learned to get through the tough times as a team and still look forward to the winning times; it teaches you about winning and losing in life.

"Those lessons have become invaluable to me," Kent continued. "I never dreamed I'd be sitting here before you, in this wheelchair. But neither do I intend to live the rest of my life confined to it. With God's guidance and help, I *will* fight the good fight, and continue to fight until one day I walk from this chair."

Throughout the room, the silence was deafening. Kent swallowed.

"It's important for me to know that my teammates still believe in me. I *need* your camaraderie. And please," Kent swallowed harder, choking back the emotion that threatened to drown him, "whatever you do, don't dwell on what happened to me, nor that the same thing could happen to you. Mine was a freak accident, an inexplicable twist of fate. Football is the greatest game in the world, and I love it with all my heart."

For a moment, Kent was stopped by the tears. He struggled for composure, attempting at the same time to will his legs to stillness. Due to the fever's stress, the muscle spasms were worse this night, causing his legs to continuously bounce up and down on the peddles. Kent was mortified. But more importantly, he was determined for no one to know of his sickness.

As he gazed out into the audience, he saw that few would notice his spasms. Everyone was crying.

"With all my heart," he continued, "I respect Coach Shof and his staff. I look forward to playing whatever role I can from the sidelines, to help turn the program at TCU around.

"At this point, I want very much to thank my parents and my family . . . for, for . . ." Kent stammered, starting once more to cry " . . . for always being there. I'd like my mom and dad and Terry Lynn, my sister, to stand now," he added, voice breaking but finally getting it out. I gotta end this, he reasoned as the crowd clapped for his family, before drowning in my own tears.

"Once again, I thank you all for this award. And for your prayers . . . and most especially, for your love."

Among clapping and tears and hugs, Kent made it through the evening, almost delirious with a fever that no one knew he had.

In May of 1975, in the throes of his third severe infection within two months, when his fever rose to 105° and would not break, Kent was taken by ambulance to Baylor Hospital. For a week, Denise again assumed the role of nurse and assured her son's survival. Finally, the urology team identified the bladder bug that wouldn't die, then killed it.

Not only did they slay the infection, but Kent learned that he had the same bug all these months. The antibiotics he ingested when his fevers mounted merely kept the infection at bay, then it waited as does a cinder to flare again into a fire. Now, rid of the bug entirely, he began to really recover. For the first time in months Kent started to feel human.

Terry Stanford drove quietly toward the Waldreps' Grand Prairie home. In the waning weeks of the spring semester, she had taken to visiting Kent every weekend. Soon school would be out for the summer, and she could spend much more time with him. Since Katie dropped from the picture and none of Kent's buddies showed an inclination to maintain ties, Terry took the sole role as friend.

This wasn't how she once thought life between them would be. She'd thought there would be more — much more — to their relations. The previous summer they had met while on a double date, each out with another. She remembered that night vividly, as she knew she always would.

Standing in front of the refrigerator at a friend's party, having drunk a bit too much wine, Terry felt a presence materialize behind her. She knew before turning that it was her sister's blind date. As often happens, those two didn't hit it off. However, Terry's and Kent's eyes met the instant she opened the door, met and locked and neither broke away for what passed like hours before Terry's own date introduced Kent.

Terry tried to avoid him at the party, but to no avail. Standing by the refrigerator, an electrical current zipped up her spine. She turned to face Kent.

70

He immediately placed an arm on either side, palms on the fridge, forming a boundary around her. Dark hair framed his handsome face, each strand perfectly in place. His hazel eyes sparkled into hers. Big and strong and in perfect condition, Kent exuded an energy known to the best of athletes. And though Terry had dated football players before, something caught her, wove a web of emotion around and through, tying her to him.

Little had she known how strong that tie would be.

They dated through the rest of the summer, keeping in touch while attending different universities. And though she treated him badly, she couldn't extricate herself from that web. Young, naive, and a virgin, Terry was set on playing the field. And through it all, Kent remained so kind and caring, in such contrast to his hulky football image. He remained persistent through all her bitchiness, and that persistence paid off. Now, after everyone with him during the limelight period of his injury had left, Terry returned. It felt like when the world comes to a loved one's funeral — all the relatives and acquaintances and everyone who claims to have loved the deceased person well. Then those folks leave and the truly bereaved are left to themselves, to endure the worst of the grieving alone.

Well, that wouldn't happen to the kindest, most sensitive boy she ever knew. Terry was here now. Somewhere in the back of her mind she always thought they would be together. But not, she reasoned now, pulling into the Waldreps' driveway, like this.

"Terry!" Denise said, hugging her after opening the door. Denise's eyes lit up, and she smiled broadly. "You look beautiful, as always," Denise said, brushing back Terry's long, dark hair.

"Hi, there," she answered. "Sorry I'm late. The traffic coming in from Nacogdoches was awful and you know how I drive, but with everybody leaving for the weekend I could hardly get out."

Kent called, "Yeah, I bet you ran most of them off the road. Texas highways won't ever be safe again."

Walking to him, Terry retorted, "Don't you give me that." She bent to kiss his forehead. Kent sat all dressed, awaiting her. He motioned to the couch's arm rest and she sat.

"How you doing, little squirrel?" he asked softly.

"Hungry?" Denise asked.

71

"Always."

Denise laughed. "You two visit and I'll finish supper," she said, disappearing into the kitchen.

Terry looked down at Kent, grasping his hand in her own. He looked so frail and white. But not nearly as bad as when she saw him the first time, six or so weeks ago. Then he looked so terrible she thought he might die.

"They got the bug," Kent said.

"For good?"

"Yep. I'll be obnoxious as ever before too long. When's school out?"

Terry frowned. "Next week. I'm gonna have to study some this weekend."

"Yeah, right," Kent replied, grinning. "Lightning will strike you for that."

"Lying, Kent, lightning strikes you for lying."

"That's what I said. Kiss me."

Terry bent and kissed his lips and then slapped his arm. "Don't be calling me a liar."

They laughed and talked and touched and kissed until supper and then continued until time for Kent's catheterization and bedtime. Terry never had seen that part of the process, so she said goodnight and left. She really did need to study, and besides, she'd be back for the whole summer next week, back to being with this boy who drew her more and more toward him.

In the living room a few weeks later, Denise said, "Well, I think we should quit it altogether." She turned a piece of catheterization equipment over in her hands. "We're not getting anything anyway."

"I wonder what else we should be doing, or not doing," Kent replied.

Denise sighed. "Who knows? They send us home with all this equipment and no instructions."

"Now, Mom, don't forget the insightful and enlightening pamphlets."

She laughed. "Oh, yeah, those have been very helpful." Other than several physical therapy booklets, some incredibly elementary pamphlets, and a hearty good luck, T.I.R.R. issued no instructions whatsoever about continued rehab. So they had catheterized once a day for the three months since arriving home. There seemed no point. Well, what the hell, Kent thought. If we don't take these matters into our own hands so to speak, we're not going anywhere.

"Sounds good to me," he agreed. "Goodbye, catheter."

"You know," Denise began, still looking at one bag. "I guess they just want you to keep buying all this stuff. Forever." She tossed her head. Kent's mom's side of the family possessed Cherokee blood — Denise's grandmother had been full Cherokee — and Denise had the high cheekbones and strong features of her ancestry. Plus, she had a take-charge attitude that Kent imagined those people perfected.

"Maybe we should do the same with all the medication, too," Kent said.

"Well, we've already weaned you off much of it. We'll just keep weaning."

Kent nodded as Denise wheeled him into the sunshine. He closed his eyes, feeling warm rays penetrate his skin. Though warned not to stay in the heat too long (his body's endocrine system, which controls heating and cooling, had also been paralyzed), the summer sun always enticed him. He and his baby sister, Terry Lynn, used to have tanning contests. He now tested his own tolerances as the Texas summer began.

And he was glad to quit the catheterization, as well as wean himself off the prescriptions. He supposed, from all the information they could glean, that he was to remain on medication forever. Pain pills and spasticity medication were abundantly supplied to spinal cord patients. He had seen too many get hooked on the drugs already. T.I.R.R. seemed to use the medication to keep the patients tranquil. Most were more than willing to comply.

Kent always had a problem with the whole drug issue, dating back to when he played high school football and drugs were starting to be the cultural rage. His feverish opposition to drug use caused lots of conflict, and the team became divided on the issue — between the "hip" guys and the uncool. But drugs had no place in athletics, and his teammates knew that if they crossed that line, they'd lose Kent's trust. This created tension and made building team unity an impossibility. Just one more nail in the coffin of those dark Alvin days.

Thinking of that now reminded Kent of his more recent teammates.

Where were they? The Grand Prairie home was only thirty-five minutes from TCU's campus. Yet only a few fellow players had visited, and not in a long while. Damn, but he needed their friendship now.

Together, he and these guys had survived sheer hell at TCU. Their freshman year was earmarked by the arrival of Attila the Hun, masquerading as the new football coach, Earl Legget. Coach Legget, a 320-pound former NFL offensive tackle, now tackled his first coaching job. His approach proved brutal.

Now, Kent always liked tough coaches who demanded 110 percent. Don Landes, his sophomore coach at Alvin, had been the best. But Attila the Earl Legget was a real madman.

Four-hour practices in 100-plus-degree heat and humidity with no water breaks were implemented to "whip our little asses into shape." Kent and two others wilted from heat strokes, hospitalized with 106° temperatures and uncontrollable spasms. Elmer, TCU's head trainer, jumped Attila's butt bigtime, and water flowed religiously thereafter.

Things had gotten so bad in August and September of 1972 that teammates plotted self-inflicted injuries to escape Legget's madness. Several departed the campus under the protection of midnight darkness, never to return. The rest survived by coming together as one to defeat a common enemy. Kent needed that rallying spirit once again.

Without them, his isolation felt fixed. But thank God for Terry. How he'd have made it the last couple of months without her he never wanted to know. He'd fallen in love the instant he saw her and now, well now he needed her desperately. And like a true soulmate and the only friend he seemed to have, Terry was there for him. Her sea-green eyes haunted him while she was away and lit up his life upon her return. He shuddered to think of the long days after summer ended and she returned to school, visiting only on weekends. At least he needn't face that for a while.

"Elmer's on the phone," Denise said, coming back out. She helped Kent into the house to cradle the receiver.

"Hey, kid, how you doin'?" Elmer asked brightly, voice gruff over the receiver. Kent thought it a beautiful voice.

"Never better," Kent lied. "You guys loafing around now that school's out?"

"Nah, working. You know us, work, work, work."

"Yeah, right," Kent answered laughing.

"But listen up," Elmer quickly began, straight to the point as usual. "Me'n Sully been figuring our own workout plan for you. You'd have to come out here three times a week and train. But we think we c'n do you some good."

Kent's heartbeat quickened.

"You feeling up to it?" Elmer asked.

"You bet. When do we start?"

"Whenever you're ready. We got the plans all done."

"How about tomorrow?" Kent asked, trying to keep his excitement at bay.

Elmer laughed. "I figured you'd say something like that. Come on out."

Kent said goodbye and returned the receiver to its cradle. He felt as if he could vault over the ceiling. If he knew Elmer and Sully, this wouldn't be any sort of token workout either. They'd push him to his limits, as he would himself. Finally!

Starting the next day, Elmer and Sully put Kent through the wringer. For two and a half hours, three days a week, the none-stop regime utilized every piece of equipment available. And it worked almost every muscle in Kent's body. In the beginning, no one knew how long or hard to work-out, so they experimented. Kent trusted Elmer and Sully totally.

The regime consisted of basic range-of-motion exercises and some weight lifting with wraparound arm weights. Kent still performed most of his weight workout at home on a mat. Of course, he made sure Terry wasn't around when he did that or she'd tease him and tie ribbons in his hair.

His favorite part of the workout was the whirlpool. TCU possessed the best-equipped training room in the Southwest Conference, complete with a giant jacuzzi. It provided the first hot bath Kent took since the injury.

The warm, bubbly waters helped lessen the involuntary muscle spasms that caused his legs to bounce around frequently. The strong jets of water also relieved tension and muscle cramps in his shoulders and neck. After twenty minutes in the whirlpool, Kent always wanted a nap.

But Elmer topped off the regime with electric shock therapy. Ultrasound machines helped treat and heal bruised and torn muscles and break up hemorrhaging within a muscle. To injured tissues they provided everything from a gentle massage to an electrically stimulated workout. Though Kent's therapy was passive, nothing had ever felt quite so wonderful and painful at once.

To watch his toes, feet, legs, fingers, hands, and arms move in every normal direction was sheer joy. And he knew it helped prevent the usual muscle atrophy that spinal cord injuries caused, as well as promote muscle strength and some bulk. After all the months of humiliation, these workouts did wonders for both body and mind.

A group of Denise and Al's friends, Betty Pettigrew, Mildred Walker, and Topsy Wright, alternated driving Kent and his mom to TCU. Again, family friends came through in the clutch. Al couldn't miss work three mornings a week, and the family could not afford a second car.

While Kent worked out with Elmer and Sully, a biblical quote kept dancing across his mind. Sometimes he recited it to the trainers. The passage came from Romans 8:28, and the part Kent quoted was "and we know that all things work together for good, to them that love God, to them who are called according to his purpose." All the time spent with Katie had bolstered his faith, and all her Bible readings lodged deeply in his brain. Katie stayed through the toughest parts, and though now she was gone, she left him closer to the Lord.

Also during this time, Kent remembered his recruitment process. The whole experience had been a kick. Coaches from all over appeared on campus, rescued him from classes, and fed him steaks. Each one promised stardom. None offered "monthly cash" or cars — as they did for the perceived blue-chippers — but all bought meals or gave tickets to the Oilers' and Cowboys' games. And bits of money — fifty to a hundred dollars — mysteriously found Kent's pockets while he visited.

As does any school kid, he liked the hoopla: the steaks, the trips to campuses, the late-night phone calls and illegal offers from key alumni.

Finally, TCU won Kent's bidding war. Tookie Berry, a junior Tri-Captain, escorted him around campus and surrounded him with pretty women and good times. Billy Tohill, a good old Southern boy and TCU's head coach, spread on the bullshit as thick as any Texas politician. The coach convinced Kent that he'd make him an All-American.

Now Kent spent his time working out at TCU, lifting weights on his own at home and sitting outside in the sun. His lifting time varied due to his sweats. The sweats plagued him daily, and he arranged his schedule around them. They were unavoidable, whether he sat up or lay down. After so many hours of sitting or being on his side in bed, the cold, clammy sweats would come. Kent loathed them.

The second variety occurred with every bowel movement. Since his bowels were paralyzed, their normal function had to be stimulated by a suppository every other morning. The procedure, which was supposed to take an hour, took three. And the sweats came with it.

As the weeks lugged on, Kent's temper wore thin. "The *part,* Mother! Get the stupid part straight."

Terry entered the Waldreps' house to the sounds of Kent's screaming. She had long since ceased ringing the doorbell.

Denise retorted, "I'm working on it."

"God, I wish I could do this myself."

Terry grabbed the comb from Denise's hand. "But you can't," she snapped. "Let me try," she said softly to Denise. Kent's mom stomped from the room.

"You're a class A jerk, Kent Waldrep," she said to him, combing the hair. Kent huffed.

"I am so sick of this," he said.

"Yeah, well so is everybody else. Where's the damn blow dryer."

Terry found it and began drying Kent's hair, wondering as she worked whether to kiss or kick him. The drying procedure gave them both a minute to cool off.

"Okay," she said, finishing. He examined his appearance in the mirror, smoothing a strand here and there, finally conceding that all looked perfect. He smiled up at her.

Shaking her head, Terry smiled back. "So," she said, "where to for lunch — I'm starved."

Kent hesitated. "I don't want to go out."

"Bull. I'm starving, and your mom's bushed. Nobody here's gonna make you anything to eat, so let's go."

"No."

For a minute, Terry stared at him. Kent, the boy who always loved to go and do, now too embarrassed by his appearance to venture out. Well, tough luck.

"Yes. Get your ass in gear and let's go." With that, she called to Denise they were going to lunch and wheeled Kent out.

His mood changed as soon as they left. He laughed and joked and prodded her. There was trouble at the restaurant, of course, with access and seating accommodations. Terry yelled at the manager until he provided suitable arrangements.

Wherever they went, men stared at her and avoided Kent's eyes. But it made him proud, she could tell, to have a pretty girl on his arm. It soothed his ego to know those same men who wouldn't meet his gaze envied him for his girl. And though he still protested about the outings, he was becoming more and more used to them. Terry refused to take no for an answer, and getting him out, coupled with the progress made through Sully and Elmer's regimes, helped Kent's confidence to slowly inch back.

Terry fed Kent a bite of steak. He chewed and smiled.

"I sure hope that nurse doesn't come back," Terry said.

"My rehab visitor?"

She nodded.

"Why?"

"She hated me."

"She didn't hate you."

Terry nodded again. "Yeah, she did. I think she was jealous. She basically told me to leave you the hell alone."

"Oh, she's just tired of me cheating on her," Kent said and grinned.

"Told me to quit giving you false hopes."

Kent frowned. "She can go to hell."

"All her hostility just made me madder, though," Terry said, feeding Kent some baked potato.

"You know," he began, shaking his head when she offered another bite, "that's part of the whole rehab system's problem. Those people're all so *angry*."

78

Terry replied, "It's their own loss of hope in life that makes them see you as hopeless."

"We'll prove them wrong," Kent said.

"You bet we will," Terry agreed as they finished and she wheeled him through the crowded restaurant where the way had to be cleared. Then they bounced down the step going out.

They spent the afternoon in the sunshine; then Denise prepared Kent for bed. Terry still hadn't participated in any of his processes, still didn't quite know what those were, didn't have a clue whether she could handle any of it herself, didn't know what there was to handle.

Denise put Kent to bed and left the bathroom light on. Terry entered his room in her pajamas. She crawled over equipment and into bed, snuggling up beside him.

In the darkness, they whispered and gossiped and giggled.

"You need to be nicer to your mother," Terry said, nibbling on his earlobe.

"I know. I know. Sometimes I just get so mad."

"I wouldn't put up with it."

"Yeah, what, you'd whip me into shape?" he asked and laughed.

"You bet."

"So start now." And for a while, they kissed as muted light from the bathroom filtered across them. They caressed one another, though not too much. Mainly, they held each other close.

And Terry felt, lying next to him, her own need for physical contact and how that was what Kent must miss as much as anything — the human touch.

"So when do you have to go back to school?"

"In a couple weeks." Kent fell silent.

"But I'll be back every weekend."

"Promise?"

"Sure."

"I love you, Terry."

"I love you, too."

For a minute they were silent. Then Kent whispered, "I'm scared."

She pulled him tighter. Emotions swirled through her, deep and flowing love for Kent, questions, fear. "I know," she said. "I am too."

Finally, Kent began to sleep. Terry lay awake in the semi-darkness, loving him, afraid to love him. Kent depended on her so — she was all he had outside the family and his parents' friends. They had been inseparable this summer, and she couldn't imagine life without him. But what would life *with* him be like?

Go to sleep, she told herself. Those are questions that don't need answering now. Besides, one day Kent would walk again, be well, and all this would be a moot point. In the meantime, she would return to school and visit on weekends. She'd make him go to football games this fall. Forever seemed a lifetime away.

"Kent," Denise began, after yet another of her son's frustrated tirades, "why don't you start a journal. You know, write about some of this. Get it down on paper. While you're sitting outside, maybe you could get some of your feelings out."

Kent huffed. He knew his parents' frustration level skyrocketed with his own. He knew they too were tired. Not only, however, was he sick to death of all this, he felt something else as well. Something he couldn't put his finger firmly on. Maybe he *should* write this out, try to sort through the ricocheting thoughts. Hell, it was worth a shot.

So as the summer wore on, Kent wrote. Long enough to identify the something else he felt. In various forms and from a variety of sources, that something was anger.

He was angry at the rehab process of T.I.R.R., which promoted dependency and discouraged hope, at rehab medicine's all-out assault on human dignity. His self-esteem and self-worth were decimated; any shred of human dignity was stolen. This process left a shell of emotions too fragile for contact with the competitive and vain outside world.

So he had called out reserve troops to outflank the teams of social workers and physiologists. But why did he have to? That system condoned a lower-than-acceptable quality of life as the standard for survivors with severe disabilities. To survive is not what life is about. Life is about thriving. And hope is *not* a dirty word.

No one or no system should be allowed to set arbitrary limits on anyone's quality of life and purpose as a human being. No one. Kent vowed to devote his life to instilling a winning spirit within the arena of spinal cord injury. Other victims and their families must be enduring the same humiliations. He just knew he could change this. There had to be a way to permeate the experience with hope and return human dignity. He would find it. Kent was angry.

And though he'd do anything to relive that day in October, Kent didn't advocate the abolishment of "amateur" football. College ball was worth playing. It returned twofold whatever one put into it. It taught precious lessons. He learned never to quit, to set goals beyond perceived limits, to be disciplined, and, most importantly, to sacrifice to win. These had saved his post-injury life already.

But when he thought about the concrete-like artificial turf on which he landed head first, Kent became angry. Would athletes' well-being ever be a major focus of sports?

And he was not angry with God. Though many might say that Kent landed the only possible way in which he could have broken his neck, he saw the opposite: he landed the *only possible way* in which he could have survived the accident. God's grace saved Kent's life. And, as it says in the quote from Romans, he knew God had a reason.

So through his anger and hostility came understanding, energy, and a new resolve to change the prospects for patients with spinal cord injuries. Who would stop him?

✧ CHAPTER FIVE ✧

WE'RE NOT LIABLE

Denise peered out her sliding glass door and into the late August sunshine. Her son sat in the shade, finally conceding some to the Texas heat. Slowly, methodically, he wrote the notes that were turning his anger into strength.

She sighed. Should she tell him more storm clouds loomed over the horizon? No, let him be for a while. Let the healing continue.

They recently returned from another stay at T.I.R.R. for Kent's six-month evaluation. It was a disaster. The focus centered on how to dress oneself. Again, the Waldreps learned nothing of value. Kent told them to just hang a sign on him that said, "Crippled son-of-a-bitch." The staff was not amused.

After that, Denise and Kent resolved never to go back and to trust their own judgments. His successes came through their initiatives anyway.

But another problem surfaced. TCU refused to pay the last T.I.R.R. bill. Something was wrong here. Dreadfully wrong.

Denise had started smelling a rat some time ago. John Wright, an attorney and a personal friend, offered to oversee the entire donation process from the beginning. TCU refused. She and Al and John found this odd, but let it go.

No correspondence came to the Waldreps; everything went through attorneys. And the attorney for TCU stated that payment for both the hospital stay and T.I.R.R. expenses had been remitted through the fund set up from public donations.

This was *not* the way things were supposed to be. The public funds raised were to go to Kent's long-range rehabilitation and living expenses. Many contributors contacted them in this regard. Of course, Kent knew nothing of the disposition and accounting of the funds, putting him in a very awkward position.

82

And it meant not only that TCU refused all responsibility in the matter, but also that the university wasn't out one cent — not even for the initial hospital stay. Kent was a scholarshiped athlete, playing in a game for TCU when the injury occurred. And TCU wouldn't even pay the hospital bill? How could this be?

During the initial crisis, TCU's chancellor gave Al his telephone credit card to enable him to keep family and friends posted on Kent's condition. Even that bill was paid from the donation fund.

When the Waldreps arrived in Birmingham that fateful October day, Chancellor Moudy assured and reassured them all would be "taken care of." They neglected to mention that this taking care meant from any and all sources except TCU.

Kent knew none of this. Denise couldn't bear to think what it would do to him: to know that not only had he been paralyzed while giving all for his team and school, but also that very school then deserted him. How to explain this?

As summer gave way to September, the Waldreps' financial picture became more bleak. Never wealthy, they had been what Denise called "comfortable." But a spinal cord injury comes with enormous expenses. And it appeared that TCU would bear none of those. Where in the world would the money come from? They were riding upon a very dangerous river, somehow keeping from being bashed upon financial rocks. But if the current were to become even a fraction more swift. . . .

Kent grew more cheerful by the day, regaining his strength, gaining a focus for his life. Though her son would never say it, Denise knew how guilty he felt. Terry Lynn had mentioned a few months before that Kent once said it might be better were he not even around. But he knew — must know — that having him alive was the most important thing in all their lives.

Now, however, Kent seemed to be putting the pieces of his life back together. And Terry Stanford brought out much of this. She brightened Kent's life like no one else. The rest of his friends deserted him, not even returning his phone calls. Everyone but Terry. And though she'd returned to school for the fall semester, her presence in Kent's life stayed secure. Without her, Kent might have buried himself in seclusion for longer than Denise cared to think about. Terry was the light that pulled Kent back.

83

But even Terry couldn't have saved Kent the morning the dam broke. His uncle, Walter Cober, delivered a letter from TCU's attorney, Marcus Ginsburg. It read:

September 25, 1975

Dear Mr. Cober:

Thank you for your letter of July 31, 1975. The slowness in response is due to the fact that I wanted to clear the matter with Dr. Moudy and the Athletic Department and the lapse of time was due to vacations and absences by various of the parties.

Let me review the various funds, financial transactions and procedures since Kent's terribly unfortunate injury. Outlays have been made from three sources: (1) TCU Athletics Department fund, (2) a gift account established at the University Bank, Fort Worth, and (3) the Birmingham fund.

(1) TCU Athletics Department funds. TCU paid all the charged hospital expenses at Birmingham, plus long distance calls charged, at Dr. Moudy's suggestion, to his personal long distance telephone number. When TCU received partial reimbursement on these outlays from Waldrep-Cober company group insurance, TCU sent the money on to Kent when the Waldreps strongly urged TCU to so do and upon their belief that this was the right thing to do. Also paid from TCU Athletics Department fund was at least one fairly recent bill received from TIRR in Houston.

(2) The University Bank fund. A fund made up of gift contributions was placed at University Bank in Fort Worth. Many of these funds arrived spontaneously, some came from a special appeal at the Cotton Bowl game, and a noteworthy number of the contributions came through the efforts of Mr. Thad Ziegler in San Antonio. Out of this fund were paid the down payment on Kent's home and one-half of the rehabilitation expenses charged by TIRR during the Houston period of Kent's rehabilitation. Initially, these funds were to be disbursed under the signatures of Frank Windegger or Abe Martin. Later, as you know, the balance

84

remaining in the fund was placed under the signature of Kent and taken from the signature of TCU personnel.

(3) The Birmingham fund. The Birmingham fund was organized and has always been controlled by Birmingham people. There was considerable delay in obtaining the first participation in Kent's expenses by the Birmingham fund, but when this participation began, the Birmingham fund paid one-half of the Houston period of rehabilitation. The Birmingham group has consistently described its goal as limited to paying not more than one-half of the medical/rehabilitation expenditures. However, subsequently there was a suggestion that the Birmingham group might want to furnish Kent a vehicle. TCU personnel have had no say in the use of Birmingham funds, which is as it should be, and has received no accounting of them.

It should be noted that TCU carried out its customary and Southwest Conference customary responsibilities in paying the hospitalization expenses of Kent. The university did not attempt to gather gift monies for this purpose or any purpose, but it was very pleased to see the ground swell of interest and support on Kent's behalf.

In the future, TCU will, of course, continue with Kent's scholarship to the level of the bachelor's degree, and Mr. Elmer Brown and his assistants will continue to work in every possible way to help Kent in his rehabilitation. However, TCU will be unable to expend any further funds from its athletics budget or its general budget.

While TCU did pay recently a bill from TIRR in the amount of $770.39, it did not intend thereby to set a precedent. Two further bills have arrived in the amounts of $964.99 and $1,105.13. The first of these is from TIRR representing charges for physician services. The second is from the general contractor, W. Blackburn, for installation of patio doors. These are being forwarded to you by Mr. Windegger.

Texas Christian University has and will always have a great concern about Kent. They earnestly hope for his very substantial rehabilitation.

If there are further questions, I promise a more prompt response.

Sincerely yours,
Marcus Ginsburg

MG:dlb
cc: Dr. J. M. Moudy
cc: Mr. Frank Windegger

Denise watched helplessly as Kent read the letter. He was crying.

Throughout the afternoon, he became more and more disconsolate. He would respond, but not until tomorrow. Her son wanted his answer to be one of heartfelt emotion, not just anger and shock.

Twenty-four hours later, Denise helped attach the hand prosthesis onto Kent's arms. She positioned him in front of the typewriter, where he practiced answering his mail.

At first, Denise watched. She watched her son, pencils taped to the prosthesis taped to each arm, as he punched the typewriter. But it was too much. Her boy had fought. He struggled and endured and never succumbed to despair. Loyalty to his school never waned. And now the very institution he fought for washed its hands of him.

Denise Waldrep turned and shuffled into her kitchen. She collapsed into a chair next to Al. Her husband, always so strong, always ready with a joke, turned a mug round and round on the table before him. When he looked at her, his brown eyes were brimming with tears.

For four and a half hours they listened to the keys echo as Kent plugged away. Tap, tap, tap, tap. For almost that entire time, Denise and Al sat side-by-side and cried.

Kent allowed his pain to temper before sitting, finally, before the typewriter. As he had read TCU attorney Ginsburg's letter, he kept hearing the reassurances given his parents by TCU chancellor James Moudy. "Don't worry, Mr. and Mrs. Waldrep. We'll take care of everything. Kent will get all the care he needs."

In less than two pages and within eleven months of his injury, Ginsburg informed Kent of TCU's decision to deny any responsibility for his injury or any present or future medical or personal needs. In short, TCU wrote off Kent Waldrep.

All he ever heard from TCU officials was that his medical bills and future needs would be dealt with. But Denise admitted that she and Al had been having trouble with the university for a while. TCU controlled the donations. Contributions were sent by fraternities and sororities at other Southwest Conference schools, TCU alums, family friends, and complete strangers with no ties to TCU or to him. People such as Lori's dad, Thad Ziegler, gave sizable amounts.

The University of Alabama, too, received a flood of donations. The Alabama Jaycees coordinated that fund-raising drive.

Alabama's response to his injury was very generous and sincere — from both the state and the university. The Waldreps never expected it, nor was the university in any way legally liable. This made their sentiment very special. And it made TCU's deception hurt all the more.

As Kent began punching out one key at a time, tears trickled down his face. Four and a half hours later, crying the entire time, his letter read:

Dear Sirs:

Thank you for the letter of September 25, 1975. The following response to that letter is strictly my own personal feelings. I feel my response is justified, due to the fact that the subject of this matter is me. May I also say at this time that although I am the subject of this controversy, I have never received any copies of the letters sent by the law firm representing TCU to Mr. Cober. Before I get any deeper into this letter I must also say that copies of this letter and all letters concerning this matter will be sent to all those people that I feel should have been sent copies in the first place. I feel that certain people at TCU that are concerned about my welfare have had no knowledge of this matter concerning the liability of the University toward my accident. It is my decision that I would like them to know why I am writing this letter, so that there will be no hard feelings between them and me over future actions.

In answering your letter may I say that I will not argue any legal points, as that will be done by those who are qualified in that field. I just wish to let it be known that I am aware of the University's feelings. I also want those concerned to know my feelings on the subject since I am the reason for the controversy.

From reading the letter dated as shown above, it becomes evident to me that two sources other than TCU contributed to the paying of my expenses. This money was sent by friends and by concerned persons of both Texas and Alabama. It is my knowledge that a fund was set up, the Kent Waldrep fund, to handle this money. It was my belief that my Father or family lawyer was in control of this money and that the money was to be used as we delegated. I never delegated control of the money to TCU or any other person or persons and since the money was sent to me, I feel I should have been informed on all matters concerning it. Many personal friends, including Thad Ziegler, sent large amounts of money to the Kent Waldrep fund under the belief that I would receive this money. To date I have received a little more than $11,000 out of the money contributed. The total amount of contributions is not known to me but at last note it was in excess of the figure which I have received. I also noted that many of these funds were disbursed under signatures other than my own or by those delegated by me to do so. This money was sent by friends and others to be used in future years as we so needed, not to repay TCU for any expenses they had incurred. Because of the nature of my "terribly unfortunate injury" I incur many more expenses than a normal person. Money, unfortunately, is the only way to pay these expenses, therefore, this is the reason for my concern over the funds. It seems unfortunate that many problems concerning these funds and liability should arise because my real concern is to walk again and not money. But my family cannot afford my expenses and I feel they are in no way responsible for the bulk of my expenses or any of them for that matter.

The Birmingham fund should have never been used for any of the expense of the injury as the other fund; because the rehabilitation was a result of the accident and it was my understanding that TCU was responsible for any expense resulting from a foot-

88

ball injury that I incurred while playing. If I had not had the rehabilitation I would still be flat on my back in the hospital, not able to move.

It was also mentioned in the letter that TCU has carried out its customary responsibilities under the Southwest Conference in paying my hospital expenses. When I signed my name on the scholarship it said nothing about limited liability and I was under the belief that all expenses would be paid by TCU if I was injured playing football. My parents were also told this by TCU coaches. I wonder how many parents would allow their sons to play if they knew they would be responsible for their son's expenses if he were injured as I was. Not many families can afford the expense or would risk it. I was never told that I was not insured and that TCU would not be responsible for such an expense as I have incurred. I also know that the present players have no knowledge of this or their parents. They are playing under the knowledge that their parents are not responsible for the expense if they are injured. Is this fair?

I appreciate the fact that TCU will continue my scholarship although I will be unable to use it unless I get much better. The therapy mentioned I feel is not a service of the University but a service extended by two very good men and friends. Although they are using TCU equipment and time, I believe they would drive to my home if I asked them to, to do the same thing. You see, they are honestly concerned and are personal friends whom I asked to help me as a friend.

As a final note before I sum up my feelings, the bills mentioned in the letter were a result of my injury, as all the bills sent to TCU have been. The patio doors were needed in case of fire, so I wouldn't burn up. Of course the chances of a fire are remote, but who would have ever thought I would break my neck playing football? What were those chances?

When I reflect on what has been said in your letter I feel guilty for breaking my neck and the expenses TCU has had because of it. That is the way I am made to feel but what I really feel is pity for those responsible for that letter and the feelings exhibited. At this point I want to state that I in no way have any ill feelings toward any of the coaching staff or athletic staff that have no control over this matter. I am sure they are completely ignorant of this matter and they have always probably been. Coach Shof has been a great friend during this whole ordeal as have all the coaches and especially Jim Garner and Elmer and Sully. They have always had my welfare first. When I chose TCU the size was a factor. I felt I would be more than just a number, I would be an individual, a person. It looks as though I was wrong. What TCU has shown me is that the expense of the school comes before the life of one of its students. I'm just a number but an expensive one who almost died for a school he represented and fought for on the football field. I wasn't the best player on the team but there wasn't another one who wanted to win more for Coach Shof than I did. If the expense of a University comes before the very life and future of one of its students then I believe the word Christian needs to be replaced by a more appropriate word. The Lord has helped me in many ways and so have other people who had no knowledge of me before the accident. I only wonder what I would have done without their help.

People like Coach Shof, Jim Garner, Elmer Brown, Sully, Thad Ziegler and the many people in Alabama and Texas that contributed money to help me and the many others that sent cards and letters, they are the ones that are concerned about me, not you who are responsible for the unfortunate controversy. At least they will be able to sleep with a clear conscience.

Kent Waldrep

Copies sent to:

Dr. J. M. Moudy	Mr. Jim Sullenger
Mr. Frank Windegger	Dr. Earl Waldrop
Mr. Marcus Ginsburg	Mr. Thad Ziegler
Mr. Jim Shofner	Mr. Tommy Bush, Alabama
Mr. Jim Garner	Mr. Walter Cober
Mr. Elmer Brown	Mr. Hogan

Emotionally spent, Kent addressed the original to James Moudy. Of all those sent copies, only Coach Shof, Thad Ziegler, and Jim Garner responded. The word from TCU was silence.

Less than two weeks later, Coach Bryant called. "Hello, son, how you doing?"

"Great Coach," Kent lied. "Working out hard."

"Glad to hear it. We don't want you loafing around."

Kent laughed. "Not me."

"Well, listen," Coach Bryant continued, "I'm calling to confirm your attendance at the TCU-Alabama game. We're all proud to be honoring you."

"What?"

"At the game," Coach Bryant said, paused, then continued, "Don't you know about this, son? We switched this year's game to Birmingham so the city and the university can honor you. The whole town's up for it. TCU confirmed all this weeks ago."

Kent swallowed. "No, sir," he replied. "TCU hasn't said a thing to us."

Coach Bryant seemed somewhat taken aback, but they talked a while longer before hanging up. The coach said to expect a call from TCU.

Ten minutes later Frank Windegger's office called, apologizing for the miscommunication. The Waldreps would be traveling on the team plane.

Hell's bells, Kent thought. As much as he wanted to publicly thank the people of Alabama for all their prayers and support, he cringed at the thought of riding on the same plane with the very TCU officials who approved the recent letter. Would life always be so damn complicated?

On the flight, Kent, Denise, and Al sat in first class. TCU's dignitaries, from the chancellor down, perched in that section as well. No one spoke. None of the players talked much either. His mom kept a smile on her face, but Kent knew that she, too, would kill to be on another plane. The silence was suffocating.

But when they arrived at the airport, everything changed. The terminal overflowed with press people and hundreds of well-wishers. "Welcome home Kent Waldrep," and "Welcome back Kent, Honorary Citizen," and other banners plastered the walls and unfurled from folks' arms. The nurses and therapists, Drs. Galbraith and Shirley, Barbara McClary, and all the Waldreps' Alabama friends greeted them.

Alabama state troopers escorted them to the Hilton Hotel, where more cheering fans met them. The next morning, Saturday, a press conference ensued. Kent felt as if he were royalty.

Troopers escorted them to the stadium, where before the game a tailgate party was held in Kent's honor. Pregame tailgate parties were common, but this one featured enormous amounts of barbecue, and a steady stream of supporters sauntered by.

They traveled to the stadium, and Coach Bryant came across the field to visit. As the game started, "Welcome Back Kent" lit up the scoreboard. The bright bulbs shone throughout the day.

More well-wishers, autograph-hunters, and photo-seekers stopped by. During halftime, Alabama officials honored Kent at midfield. How odd, Kent thought — our lawsuit against the artificial turf company is being filed as I'm being wheeled across this concrete-like field. But this was not a day for negativity, and the thought was fleeting.

They presented to him a Vulcan bronze (a replica of the huge statue that overlooks Birmingham). They showered him with gifts, including the game ball. Sixty thousand people gave him a standing ovation. Sitting ten yards from where the injury occurred, Kent felt Alabama's caring cloak him. And through his tears, he felt at home.

For the entirety of his time in the state, Kent basked in the glow of Alabama's love.

The Waldreps returned to Texas bolstered by warm memories. They later learned TCU made more money playing in Alabama because of increased attendance, but Kent refused to believe this was the deciding factor in TCU's switching the game to Birmingham.

However, TCU never honored Kent at a game. And only through the efforts of Jim Garner, TCU Sports Information Director, did Kent get a reserved special seating area in the press box at Amon Carter Stadium in 1975.

TCU's attitude became increasingly, "if we pretend the Waldreps don't exist, perhaps they'll go away." But Kent wasn't about to go away. His injury would not stop him, and neither would TCU's injustice. He might be down, but in no way was he out. Kent Waldrep had way too much living left to do.

✧ CHAPTER SIX ✧

CROSSROADS

"I miss you in a weird way," Terry's letter stated. "You're always on my mind."

Kent reread her words for the umpteenth time. She wrote regularly, and this served to keep her close. Of course, she visited every weekend, but as autumn leaves faded to brown and fell he missed her more and more. Without Terry, oh, well, he didn't want to think about it.

She'd taken him to his first TCU football game and almost turned-over his wheelchair while pushing him from the elevator. Kent had laughed, and the memory still amused him, though Terry was mortified. Even now he couldn't tease about it without her smiles turning to frowns.

But she had brightened last weekend when he relayed to her a recurring dream — the one where he was running.

"On your own legs?" Terry had asked, her brown head backlit by the warm November sun, causing a halo to radiate around her. "You yourself were running?"

"Yeah," Kent replied. "Like I'm on the track team. But I'm just learning to run. It starts out real slow, like, like — "

"A train?"

Kent nodded. Terry often finished his sentences, as if they shared the same mind. "It begins with a major effort, a giant push, and then slowly, slowly I start off, gaining speed, and before you know it, whoosh." He raised his right arm forward.

Terry stared at where his arm had lifted then lowered as if still seeing the movement, and once again, Kent felt proud of his progress. Though he wasn't yet in the shape he desired, he had regained lots of strength.

"Then it's just a matter of time," Terry said, nodding her strong chin forcefully. "That's a sign. You'll walk again. I just know it." Wafting across the warm breeze, her perfume reminded Kent of his grand-

93

mother's asters, which once bloomed this time of year. The aroma was strong and heady and sweet.

They laughed and kidded the rest of that day, and now, staring out at the norther-induced blue of the sky, Kent missed her terribly.

He set the letter down and picked up his Bible, opening it to Ephesians and the passages he was studying. They centered on Christ's purpose on earth, and the purpose God has for each of His children. Kent was not yet certain what God had in store for him but knew it would be revealed in due time. For now, the holidays approached quickly, bringing Terry home for break. How much better this Christmas would be than last! The sights and sounds of the season made him smile as he dove into his study.

And that Christmas *was* 180° from the last dismal one spent at T.I.R.R. The memory of Charles Fox and himself plotting, failing, and then reaping small rewards last New Year's Eve faded with Terry's kisses as the clock struck midnight; 1976 promised to be a banner year.

One evening in the middle of January, Al breezed into the house. His booming voice filled the air before Kent saw the fit man enter, more agitated than usual.

"Take a look at this, son," Al said, dropping a folder into Kent's lap and then fidgeting from one foot to the other.

Laboriously, Kent opened the top and poured the contents into his lap, picking up pieces of paper, one by one. From the beginning, Al had insisted Kent do everything possible for himself.

"What'cha think of that?" Al asked, voice rising.

"Let me look at it before I say," Kent replied, grinning. He'd better hurry though. Al seemed in no humor to wait.

Enclosed in the folder were news clippings concerning the Russian approach to treatment of spinal cord injuries. And photos. Photos of Americans who had traveled to Leningrad for treatments, some of whom now could walk.

Kent looked up. His father's eyes were dancing in that ruggedly handsome face. It was the most excited Al had been in, well, a long, long while.

Since the injury, Denise had provided the primary care for Kent. Everyone preferred it that way. Kent and his father would've clashed

94

badly, and while he could get away with tongue-lashing his mother in his frustration, Al wouldn't have stood for it.

But that didn't mean his dad wasn't right there in the trenches. And for the past many months, Al had been quietly searching for answers, any kind of answers, for a thread of hope that said research *was* being conducted somewhere, that the entire world hadn't written off spinal cord injuries.

"They're using enzyme injections and hyperbaric oxygen treatments. And Kent," Al said and paused. For an instant, his eyes grew moist; then he cleared his throat and continued, "they're getting results."

"Wonder what the U.S. doctors think?" Kent asked, more to himself than anyone.

"Dunno," Al replied. "But I'm getting letters off tomorrow to the U.S. Department of Health and some others. I'll write Dr. Carter at T.I.R.R., too, and this Oregon neurologist — Tunturi. Denise," Al said, rising and bounding into the kitchen, "look at this."

Kent listened for a time to the hum of their voices, a feeling of lightness engulfing him. Who knew what this could bring, but finally a road to take, a ray of optimism for the family to focus upon. God knew they needed one.

The past months had taken an enormous toll on his folks, and though they tried to hide it, their relationship was now anything but normal. The Waldreps had always been a close-knit group. And his accident, rehab, and the ensuing year had bonded the family in a way in which nothing else could. But the ordeal also opened a chasm so wide between his parents that Kent wondered if it could ever be bridged.

He sensed rather than reasoned that their problems all circled back to him. How painful it must be for a mother to watch her boy like this! How helpless a strong man must feel when looking upon his paralyzed son and seeing no action to take. How pervasively that must enter into every facet of their lives. Well, together they had made it this far; with God's grace they could make it another mile. Then another. And on down the road.

For the next three months, Al wrote constantly. He wrote the U.S. Department of Health, Education and Welfare. He wrote T.I.R.R. and University Hospital in Alabama for Kent's medical records. Dr. Galbraith from University sent them immediately. It took Al two months,

95

numerous letters and phone calls, and finally a personal visit to extract the records from T.I.R.R. (for which they charged him). Dr. Carter himself brushed off all references to Russia.

The U.S. Institute of Health in Bethesda, Maryland, referred Al to Dr. Steponov, the Counselor of Medicine, Embassy of the Soviet Union, in Washington D.C. Al wrote, sending along Kent's medical records. From the start this bode for a long, red-tape filled struggle. Fine, Kent thought. We'll wade through.

Kent corresponded with Dr. Tunturi, the research scientist and anatomy teacher at the University of Oregon Health Sciences Center. Dr. Tunturi was currently researching nerve regeneration and had traded information with the Soviet doctors concerning the enzyme and hyperbaric oxygen treatments. No, these were not available in the U.S. — the FDA hadn't approved them. But Dr. V. U. Ugryumov, director of the Polenov Neurosurgical Institute in Leningrad, *was* having some success. Of course, Tunturi emphasized, most successful surgery and therapy is done immediately after the injury and before scar tissue begins to form and hinder regeneration of the nerve and spinal cord. The treatments, however, provided a chance at any stage. It wasn't a good chance, he stressed. But it was the only one.

Al received word from the Department of State in April. This would take time. Also in April came a letter from the Department of Health, Education and Welfare stating that "the capabilities of the Polenov Institute are no better than those at spinal cord injury centers in this country."

Says who? Kent thought. Those same professionals who adamantly stated, "Regeneration of the spinal cord is impossible" and therefore research is unnecessary? Those stone-cold gurus of higher thinking?

Also in April, Kent finally met Governor George Wallace face to face, on the campaign trail in Dallas. Kent went at the governor's request, and Wallace told the press that meeting Kent was the highlight of the stop.

Kent, too, remained in the news. The media had gotten wind of the Waldreps' delving into alternative treatment and the possibility of traveling to Russia. No one but the AMA seemed to think the idea anything but hopeful.

Spring drifted into the dripping-hot days of June. Terry stayed in

96

Nacogdoches for summer school. Back to looking more like his old self, Kent traveled more easily outside. Although he'd quit working out at TCU — all the legal unpleasantness had left him too uncomfortable to stay — he'd started a program with Parkland Hospital, and his strength continued to increase. Though his former buddies never returned his phone calls, he still had Terry and all his family and their friends. Terry cautioned him not to take his companions' desertion too hard, for we get but few true friends in this life. It merely required a crisis to sift the wheat from the chaff.

That summer, too, Barbara McClary and her family came to visit. Though they kept in touch by phone and Barbara's husband had lodged with the Waldreps several times while passing through Texas, this was the first time the entire McClary clan came to stay.

Petite but fit, Barbara helped with Kent's passive range-of-motion exercises, spelling Denise, who stood watching. As yet another of those tremendous muscle spasms engulfed him, they stopped a second.

Her eyes clouded and a frown passed over her face. He was used to seeing this, but Barbara wasn't.

"It's okay," Kent reassured her. "Don't worry, they pass."

As they finished, the doorbell rang, and Denise greeted another visiting Waldrep friend.

"This is Barbara McClary, Mildred," Denise began. "She saved Kent's life."

They all talked and sipped iced tea, until it was time for Mildred to go. Denise walked her out, leaving Kent and Barbara alone.

"Your parents have accomplished so much here," Barbara said, looking around the house. "It's overwhelming how much they've been able to do, to rearrange and make things accessible."

Kent nodded. "It's been a real burden on them, though they won't let on."

"You're no burden, Kent," Barbara said and smiled. "Losing you, now that would be a burden." Her eyes misted, and Kent felt the tears in his own.

"You miss him real bad," he said.

Barbara swallowed and then said, "It's helped me to understand what your mother is going through. To lose a child..." Her voice drifted off.

97

Her pain stabbed his heart. Six months before Kent's accident, Barbara's three-year-old son had been kicked in the head by a horse. Twelve hours later, he died.

"But God always gives back," Barbara said. "It was after that accident that I returned to teaching. I was teaching electrocardiography, anatomy and physiology, and medical terminology to paramedics. I figured I'd better become a paramedic myself if I was going to teach them."

Kent asked, "There aren't many R.N. paramedics, are there?"

"I was the first," Barbara said. "And thank God. When you hit the turf and didn't move, I could get to you faster than anyone else."

Laughing, Kent said, "Yeah, I'da had them taking my helmet off if you hadn't gotten there. Not to mention, I'da suffocated."

Barbara cocked her strawberry-blond head. Through glasses, her eyes looked warmly at him. "You know, Kent, I wouldn't have known not to remove your helmet without the paramedic training. And I wouldn't have had that if I hadn't gone back to teaching.

"I don't know why Kellen died," she said and paused before continuing, "but if he died so I could learn to help save you, then that's why."

Kent reached to touch her arm with the back of his hand. So special, this woman was.

He swallowed hard and said, "You did save my life, Barbara."

"No," she answered. "Your mother humbles me by introducing me that way."

"But she's right," Kent said.

Again Barbara shook her head. "I didn't save your life, Kent. God did. I was just God's hands in that situation."

For the rest of the week, Kent and Barbara talked. They talked of what was new in therapy, of what was on the horizon. They spoke of Russia and hope. When the McClarys loaded up and left for Alabama, a hole opened in Kent's heart the size of Texas.

The next day he received a letter from Terry. His heartbeat quickened as his mother handed him the envelope. Just what the doctor ordered.

She spoke of mundane things and told him to look on the bright side again. Then the tone of the letter took a downward turn.

There's just some sort of weird vibrations I get when I'm around you. I know you're having trouble understanding things. But sometimes we take too long trying to understand things we couldn't ever, and then we lose sight of some of the most important things around us. I could never imagine what hard times you're going through. But I try and even though I'm far away, not just in Nacogdoches but even sometimes when I'm with you, remember I'm still with you.

Of course, I don't like seeing you the way you are — but like others, I won't stay away. Friends don't ever give up and they should always see the inside no matter how hard it is for them to understand.

So, sweetie pie, you keep pitchin' — try hard.

Love, Squirrel

One of the sweats seemed to be coming on, though Kent had not been sitting long. But his arms felt cold and clammy, and perspiration broke out along the back of his neck. *You know I hate seeing you like this.* How often had he heard those words? Or heard that was why friends didn't visit?

Kent could sense when folks felt uncomfortable around him. He wanted to scream at them, "I need love and understanding, not pity or sympathy!" And to help put people more at ease was one reason he worked out so hard — to get back into a shape that appeared normal. He knew that until he could walk again, he'd never completely be part of the "normal" world. But the better he looked, the stronger he was, the more he could do, then the more accepted he would be.

One day a doorman unabashedly studied him, finally asking, "What's a good-looking guy like you doing in a wheelchair?" Kent's chest had swelled as he politely answered. Kent did all he could to make things easier on the "normal" world and still, so many shunned him.

He could take it from the outside, but from within his inner circle? From Terry? And wasn't it ironic that her distance came at the very time *he* felt capable of truly loving someone?

Sure, he had fallen in love many times before the accident, had presented all his deepest feelings and left himself open and vulnerable.

99

Thank God for that. Those experiences helped him now to depend upon others — mainly Al and Denise — to rely on them and himself. He would have loved to trust in friends, too, but they "couldn't stand to see him like this," so he cut off ties to the rest of the world. He felt somewhat like a self-sustained island.

But Terry. He'd counted on Terry, not that he thought the dependence fair. Other girls said that Terry loved him out of sympathy or pity, though he knew that wasn't true. Terry loved him. She felt guilty about dating other guys, even though he urged her to. She stuck by him and spent so much time with him, when no one else his age would. But she repeated, more often than not these days, "I wish you'd hurry up and get well."

Any hint of marriage had flown south for the winter. What, did she think he would walk tomorrow?

They'd had a nasty argument last weekend when he tried to explain his feelings.

"But I'm not looking for a girl to fall in love with, not till I'm well," Kent had said.

Terry stared at him, dark eyes growing large and luminous in the muted light of sunset. "Kent," she began, "I don't want to — "

"Date. Go on, go out."

"You want me to fall in love with someone else?"

"Whatever," Kent lied. "I know you don't want to miss out."

"You're full of shit," Terry said, voice wavering. "You don't want to feel guilty about me, but you don't want anybody else having me either!" In tears she had stormed out.

Okay, there *was* some truth there, though he'd never admit it aloud. His feelings for Terry churned round like margaritas mixing in a blender. He loved the girl, but a commitment to him would require a responsibility even he couldn't fathom.

That person would be making a great sacrifice, so the decision must be hers. He would not sway anyone his way. If a girl came along who could love him as he was, be satisfied with him and no other, she had to say it. He would not apply pressure on anyone.

So if Terry truly loved him as *is*, she should know the things he hadn't said. And though she repeated, "When you get well," and "If you were well," she never said, "It doesn't matter if you walk or not."

100

Once she was in love with him. But other people, his "condition," and his own hesitation ruined it. He refused to let on how he wished she'd date only him, nor would he venture talk of marriage, since she obviously neither understood nor accepted the accident — not in the way a wife must.

Still, Terry was his best friend, and he couldn't stand to forfeit that friendship. So he prodded her to date. He pushed her away to keep her close. It made no sense, but what other choice was there? He truly resented others' inability to accept his "condition," and Terry remained despite it all. He could not lose that. Even if it meant sacrificing her romantic love.

Older people such as Lindy Berry and Jim Garner from TCU were his friends now. He had his parents' and sisters' love. And he had God. As the summer of '76 turned into fall, Kent continued to write out his feelings, to mull over TCU's failed responsibility, to ponder his future, and to pray.

"What they're saying, Kent," Denise began, "is that if we sue TCU, it could have an adverse effect on the artificial turf lawsuit."

Kent stared at his mother. "I don't get it," he replied. "One screws up the other?"

"I guess," Denise said, shaking her head and staring at the lawyer's letter. "If we don't sue the artificial turf company, then they'll lay down defective turf again and this kind of injury may happen again. Mr. Hogan seems to think anything against TCU would have 'adverse effects.'"

Kent rubbed his chin with the back of his hand, saying, "Well, I really don't want to sue TCU in the first place. But they've denied any responsibility and that's not fair. I don't want *that* to happen to anybody else either."

Denise sighed. "I know."

"If all the schools in the Southwest Conference would contribute equally to a special fund, even an insurance fund that provided for all expenses to an injured athlete with spinal cord damage, none of this would be necessary."

Denise put her fists on her hips. "I still can't believe they had no insurance for this. I'm sure they'll get it now."

"We can only hope," Kent replied. "Hell, I can't imagine suing TCU anyway. It's my school. My team."

"I know."

She left him outside in the autumn sunshine, walking into her kitchen to start supper. When Al arrived, they considered legal alternatives, and decided not to pursue anything against TCU, though the university had left them high and dry.

At the end of October, two years after the injury, their attorneys sent a letter confirming that the Waldreps would not file suit against TCU. Denise and Al both felt uneasy about the entire situation but decided in the end to trust their legal counsel. What else could they do?

Also at the end of October, Al received news from the Russians, as they had come to be known in the household. There was a possibility of Kent getting into the Polenov Institute. A myelogram was requested. The Waldreps were ecstatic and scheduled an appointment with Dr. Kemp Clark, chief of neurosurgery at University of Texas Southwestern Medical School and Parkland Hospital.

Al, Denise, Kent, and his sister Terry Lynn sat expectantly in Dr. Clark's office. Al fidgeted, crossing one leg, uncrossing, crossing the other. Terry Lynn rose and paced. Denise watched them as Kent sat statue-still.

Dr. Clark kept them waiting an hour, but Denise had grown used to such delays. Neurosurgeons were funny people. Still, she hoped this wasn't an omen of things to come.

"Good afternoon," Dr. Clark said, bustling in. He sat immediately and began shuffling papers.

All the Waldreps greeted him, though the doctor didn't look up.

"Dr. Clark," Al began, shifting in his seat. "I assume you know the reason we're here."

Dr. Clark shot a glance up at Al and then returned to his papers.

Al continued, "We've heard from the Polenov Institute in Russia. There is some chance of Kent being admitted, and they've requested — "

Dr. Clark waved a hand through the air and said, "A complete waste of time."

Al swallowed hard and sat back in his chair. Kent began, "But Doctor — "

"Why are you people wasting your time and energy like this," Clark stated more than asked.

"Because there's hope," Terry Lynn blurted before anyone else could speak. She stood behind Kent, both palms on his shoulders. Her knuckles were white. Denise knew her daughter appeared waif-like, but to underestimate her tenacity would be a mistake.

Dr. Clark glanced sideways at Terry Lynn, and his upper lip seemed to curl. "They play on the hopes of people like you," he said. "There is no hope in situations such as this. There are no answers."

"Why don't you let us find that out for ourselves, Doctor," Al said, and Denise marveled at his restraint. Al was not famous for that trait.

"And subject the rest of America to your false hopes? Please."

"While we respect your opinion, *Doctor,* that's not why we're here," Al said. "We are merely requesting a myelogram."

"No."

Al's ruddy face turned dark.

"But Dr. Clark," Denise began, "we're just requesting a hospital service, that's all. We want a simple test."

"No. I will not be a part of this absurdity. If anything, the Russians are decades *behind* us."

Terry Lynn ran from the room, slamming the door behind her.

"That will be all," Dr. Clark said, rising.

"You mean you won't give us the medical test?" Kent asked. He stared directly at the neurosurgeon, as his square jaw dropped.

"Of course not. This is a waste of all our time." And with that, he walked out.

Denise felt the air leave her lungs. What? Not even a simple test?

They left and gathered up Terry Lynn who sat outside crying in rage. "How can he do that? Arbitrarily make those kinds of judgments?" she asked.

Al remained silent. Only Denise and Kent spoke on the ride home, voicing their disbelief and anger.

103

As they reached home Al said, "Don't worry, son. Minor setback." He winked at Kent in the rear view mirror.

"I know, Dad."

So Al busied himself finding a neurosurgeon to administer the test. But by Christmas he still hadn't found one. What was the deal here?

Denise spent the week before Christmas cooking. All the family would be in, Terry Lynn and her boyfriend, Brad, Carole and her husband, Larry. Carole was pregnant, and Denise hardly had time to think about her first grandchild's arrival. Her daughters' lives seemed as if from another world. Guilt pricked at Denise's skin. Terry Lynn, so young, growing serious about Brad, life paths stretching out before her, needed her mother. And there just wasn't quite enough of Denise to go around. Perhaps one day her daughters would understand.

For now, Denise was too busy squeezing the lead out of every nickel. This would be a season of scant gift-giving, but with family and friends gathered, who cared? And Terry Stanford would be here for Kent.

A rift had grown between those two, and both suffered for it. Terry's sad eyes told more than her words; Kent's loneliness, more than his denials.

Dear Lord, if they just weren't so young. Kent kept pushing Terry to date. When the girl complied, he grew angry. Terry didn't choose to go out; she did so on Kent's insistence and then felt very guilty. Kent no longer knew how much Terry loved him. Nor did he comprehend that he would never shake free of loving her.

But marrying Kent required more than any young girl could fathom; caring for a spinal cord injury was absolutely unknowable until one has done so. Terry hadn't a clue. A bright, beautiful, vivacious girl, Terry had her whole life spread wide before her. Could she afford to stay with Kent forever? Could she afford not to? Which choice created the truest prison? Denise vowed to talk with her at some point during the holidays. One way or another, the child's suffering must be eased. And it had become increasingly obvious that Kent wasn't able to help. Her son was a young man in love — difficult under the best of circumstances. And these were not the best of circumstances.

✧

104

Terry Stanford approached the Waldreps' driveway with some trepidation. Lights on the Christmas tree winked from the window. A beautiful handmade cedar wreath hung on the front door. The whole world glowed with holiday cheer. But somewhere in the past few weeks, she had lost her Christmas spirit. Or had it ever existed?

She sat for a time in her car, surrounded by so many other friends' cars. The Waldreps were her family; she loved them as such. She and Terry Lynn were good friends. Denise and Al were like surrogate parents. And she felt connected to Kent in a way that felt like forever. But God, what about the rest of her life? *Could* love conquer all?

She and Kent never spoke of love anymore. He had grown increasingly distant, and yet his dependence on her intensified daily. The more he needed her, the more he pushed her to date others and the more she ran.

And marriage? Can I take care of him, she wondered? Can I *do* it? Unless something changed, Kent would never have children. No children. And, she was still a virgin. What if...? Dear *God*, what do I do?

Terry still sat as the front door opened and Denise walked outside, peering into the scarcely lit drive. "Terry?" she called. "Is that you?"

"Yep," she answered, bounding out. The last thing she wanted was for Denise to worry. Kent's mother had enough on her mind.

"I was just getting my stuff all gathered up," she said, grabbing presents and hauling them in. Denise hugged her and two of the presents dropped to the sidewalk. They laughed.

"Here, let me help. Kent asked a minute ago where you were." Denise picked up the presents and into the house they went, into brightly colored, twinkling lights and the spicy-sweet smells of cloves simmering that lingered atop the pungent aroma of pine needles. Laughter filled the house, and hugs touched her heart. In the sparkle of Kent's eyes gazing up at her, all fears vanished and they kissed as if reunited after years of separation. Al brought her a steaming mug of hot-spiced rum. For a while in the Waldreps' living room, amid tall tales and warm drinks and the cozy feel of Christmas, Terry felt safe and warm and loved.

There were lots of toddies that night, lots of good cheer. Folks came and went. She and Terry Lynn sneaked into the bedroom for girl-talk. As they emerged, Denise entered and motioned for Terry to stay.

"I've been wanting to talk with you," Denise began, sitting on the bed. Terry sat beside her. "I know how difficult a time you're having. I know Kent keeps pushing you to date."

Terry nodded. Denise was so strong. So in control. How on earth did she do it?

"I know you're having trouble with it."

Terry tried but could not keep the tears from welling in her eyes. "I hate this," she said, mouth quivering. "I go out with other guys and think of Kent. I stay home and think my life is passing by. I don't know what to do." She began to cry.

Denise wrapped an arm around her. "It's okay. It's okay. Kent doesn't know, he doesn't know how to deal with all this either. But he loves you, Terry. *That,* I'm sure of."

Through tears, Terry nodded. "I love him, too."

"I know. And I love you like a daughter. There's no one I'd rather have as my daughter-in-law than you. Kent needs you. I need you. We all love you. But these decisions can't be based on love alone. There's so much at stake.

"You live your life," she continued. "Try and deal with Kent the best you can — I know how difficult he's being. He's doing the best he can, too, though sometimes I want to shake him." Denise paused. "But you *must* know that whatever happens, I'll love you just the same."

For a while they cried together, then dried their eyes, and returned to the party.

Terry didn't stay long after that and besides, it was late. As she began driving home, nausea engulfed her. She pulled to the side of the road three times, the sickness rising up.

Later lying in bed, she stared at the ceiling. That she would always be in love with Kent Waldrep was certain. Maybe all really would work out. Maybe God had some master plan He just hadn't revealed yet. But how to tell him, or Denise for that matter, that she had actually come to *like* the guy she now dated? For the first time, she had allowed herself feelings for someone besides Kent. With this new guy, she was happy and life almost seemed normal. As she drifted into fitful sleep, a silent prayer passed repeatedly over her lips, "Please, God, please. Help me."

CHAPTER SEVEN

ONE STEP AT A TIME

Terry Lynn did not return to school that January but instead stayed home in Grand Prairie to plan her wedding. Though she was marrying Brad, one of Kent's best high school buddies, the boys had drifted into different interests during college. Still, they remained friends. His sister's happiness warmed the atmosphere. Her blue eyes sparkled in her delicate face as she planned and worked. She laughed a lot.

Around the middle of January, Kent received a letter from Terry Stanford. Again she started with school-life stuff. And once more, a different tone surfaced by page two:

> I'm sorry I've been so weird actin' these past few months. You're still the best friend I've ever had in my whole life. I guess now it's hard for me to think of the way we were once. I guess that's why I've been kinda weird. You know how I am anyway. For a while there I couldn't think of anyone but you and that wasn't fair to me or you — like we decided. So as you know it was hard for me to ever get close to anyone because your thought always came into my mind. But finally I became realistic as you always told me to be. It wasn't until this year that I finally started liking someone. I had dated him since last Feb. and hadn't really given in to liking him till this September. I finally told myself I could do this and still have you being very special to me as you always had been, and I knew you would want this for me as you always had said. I had a big talk Thanksgiving with my mother, grandmother and daddy. I told them about how I was feeling guilty for not telling you I was dating someone steadily and that it was really bugging me. Mom said you would be happy for me and that someday when I marry — whomever that poor soul might be — you would be on the front row. I guess I felt weird all during Christmas — I wanted

to tell you so much and then I wouldn't ever find the opportunity. I felt we weren't as close as we used to be talking so much, and felt it to be my fault. So now I feel a ton better. Please, Kent, for my sake don't ever think I'm not there, no matter what, 'cause I still am even though I haven't been as good of a friend as I should have been. You have been the most influential person in my life and I feel lucky you came along my way.

You keep out of trouble and I'll see you soon!

Always — Squirrel

Vanished air left Kent's lungs a vacuum, but only for time. He knew Terry was dating, but not that she actually *liked* the guy. Well, she'd come back, sooner or later.

Through the winter and into the early spring of 1977, they often spoke by phone. Terry called with boy troubles, and Kent christened her a princess.

"Don't take abuse, Terry," Kent often said, "of any kind. You deserve better. Get up on that pedestal where you belong."

Oddly, this wasn't as painful as others thought. With his own life so topsy-turvy, he needed Terry's friendship most of all. And she needed to explore what else was out there.

Finally that spring, Al found a neurosurgeon willing to perform the myelogram — but only under the guise of anonymity. Denise kept commending both her husband and son for their new-found patience. Patience seemed, at this point, Kent's designated lesson from God.

So he received the myelogram and off went its results. Correspondence between the Waldreps, the State Department, and the Polenov Institute heated up, but still months passed between letters. An associate professor of Russian at TCU, John Loud, translated the Russian correspondence for them. More months passed between dispatches. About the time the silence made Kent antsy, new word would arrive.

In April, Al contacted Jim Wright's office, and the Fort Worth Congressman's staff jumped into the middle of negotiations.

Although the U.S. doctors constantly and publicly pummeled the idea of alternative treatments, Russia, and all of Kent's efforts, his own confidence in the trip — his hopefulness — never waned. It seemed the closer the venture came to reality, the more threatened the U.S.

doctors and the AMA became, and the more they discounted — in print — any hope. The *National Enquirer* ate it up. But so did most major dailies and magazines. Kent Waldrep's desire to travel to Russia for treatments that were unavailable in the U.S. plopped a fly in American medicine's soup. As his quest continued, the professional response grew progressively more scathing.

In late March, Kent spoke to TCU's Fellowship of Christian Athletes. Two and a half hard years after his accident, in the midst of a paper-trail struggle to get to Russia for treatments, with both of his folks now working to make ends meet, Kent spoke to a Christian group at the very university that disowned him.

He began by commending the fantastic work done by the FCA and stressing the importance of Christian fellowship. "I have been fortunate to have the pleasure of growing in my young Christian life with the fellowship of people like Lindy Berry, Tim Pullium, Jim Garner, Coach Shof, and the guys in FCA here at TCU. If there's one thing I want to emphasize about FCA and athletics, it's that they break down all social and racial barriers in a way that nothing else in this country can. In athletics as in FCA, you work for a common goal. You don't think about the color of the guy that's handing off the ball to you; you're both working to reach the same goal. It's kind of neat and all athletes share this feeling. FCA helps to build this bond even stronger."

He spoke for a while about God in his life, about God's grace concerning his accident, and the peace that developed from that. He talked of situations where it became difficult to see God's guidance and of walking in faith.

"My injury slowed me down from fourth gear to neutral. But only when God has become a part of every phase of your life have you really accepted Him. And when God comes into your life, He's with you always. Believe me, He never slept a wink while I was hospitalized.

"In closing," Kent said, "I'd just like to say that God has given me, in my circumstances, the will to fight when some say why. He has shown me that it's *not* His perfect will that I sit in a wheelchair. He's given me a new and clearer perspective on my life. Christ can help you, too, in your own circumstances. Just ask."

The audience gave him a standing ovation. Kent enjoyed the lunch immensely.

109

Jim Garner, director of TCU's Sports Information, called out to Kent as the meeting broke up: "Can I talk with you a minute?"

"Sure," Kent answered, wheeling slowly toward him. Jim remained a good friend these past years.

"I've just been granted the authority to add a new position in Sports Information. It's an assistant S.I.D. You interested in the job?"

"You sure that isn't Assistant S.O.B.?" Kent joked and then added quickly, "What do I do? When do I start?"

Jim laughed. "Windegger and I will come visit with you tomorrow."

"This your idea or his?" Kent asked, his mind reeling. He couldn't imagine Windegger initiated this.

"A mutual decision, pal. Let's talk tomorrow. You still working at the mortgage company?"

Kent nodded. He'd been working for his uncle's mortgage company, collecting overdue house payments. But now, man, a real job.

"We'll come there then. See you tomorrow."

The next day, Jim Garner and Frank Windegger laid out Kent's job description. He would cover games, help out the sports journalists, and write copy as well. And he'd be announcing at games. They set up immediate rehearsals for the P.A. systems at the stadium and the coliseum. He would begin April 1, 1977. April Fools, TCU!

The situation was complicated, but they figured it out. With Dad having to drive, getting Kent there and back every day would be tricky. But hell, the family could use the money.

Oh, man, a sports-writing job! And some game commentating. Yeah, Monday Night Football! Wait'll I tell Terry.

He returned home and called her. They talked about the new job and Brad and Terry Lynn's upcoming nuptials. They laughed and teased until by the time Kent said goodbye, it felt like old times. Romance with Terry wasn't yet dead, though God alone knew its path. One way or another, this wedding should prove very interesting.

Terry Stanford stood in the back room of the chapel, breathing deeply to steady her nerves. Why she felt so "on stage" at Terry Lynn's wedding, she hadn't a clue.

110

"My two Terrys," Denise said, wrapping an arm around each of them.

Terry, Terry Lynn, Denise, and another of the bridesmaids had already broken into tears once and were forced to stop everything and redo all makeup.

"Don't start," Terry said and Denise laughed.

How beautiful mother and daughter were, standing side by side. Terry Lynn, in the Cinderella gown with her long, highlighted hair swept back, looked like a real princess. Maybe Kent meant his sister was the fairy tale heroine all along.

They had such fun the last few days, through the rehearsal and dinner and the partying afterward. She and Kent would return down the aisle together — she a bridesmaid, he a groomsman. It almost seemed as if it were the two of them getting married.

And how she loved him. That quarterback she now dated couldn't hold a candle to Kent. Damn it all. Their fierce connection grew stronger with each passing year. Would she ever get over him? Why the hell *not* just marry him?

Terry took a deep breath. It was time to walk down the aisle.

The ceremony was brief but beautiful. Kent read some verses but Terry missed the words. She was too caught up in the resonant sound of his voice, the strong yet gentle tone she heard nightly in her dreams.

The groom kissed the bride and then came the wedding march, and Terry Lynn and Brad floated away, followed by the other attendants. Terry and Kent were last to leave.

Slowly, she pushed him down the aisle, not noticing the people still seated, until at the end of the rows a sharp corner loomed. Shit, they hadn't rehearsed this. Terry carefully maneuvered the chair into position and then curved at just the right instant. All eyes watched them. And everyone was crying.

Through the reception and the all-night party afterward, Terry kept close to Kent. The touch of his hand, the feel of his skin under her fingers, the sweetness of their kisses wove another web around her. To leave this man again — how could she? Had this wedding been hers and Kent's? No, she reminded herself all that night and into the following weeks. No. She and Kent had not wed, not voiced any vows nor signed any papers.

And then Kent sent a photograph of himself, looking happy and strong and fit. He signed it, "To my future wife, Terry. Love, Kent."

Terry bolted outside, into the rising Texas heat. She ran. Legs churning, lungs afire, the city streets became a wavy-heated blur. It was no use — Kent's face hovered in front of her. Exhausted, she stopped, dropped to the curb, and cried.

After all that had passed, she possessed no more answers than in the beginning. Could she care for him in reality? Hell, she *still* didn't know what that reality consisted of. Sure, she could coax him through the tough times, be his cheerleader. But care for him day to day? Could she *do* that?

Trudging back into her apartment, sweaty, tired, tear-soaked, Terry sat on the couch and stared at the carpet. For the rest of that day, she watched each spiraled pattern circle back to its center, following every route as if the nucleus of one would have The Answer. But not one path pointed the way.

Kent was having a wonderful time with his new job. The summer's slower college season provided a little breathing space, and he'd settled into a nice work routine by the time classes started again in August. Damn, but it was nice to be *productive* again. His only unease stemmed from working for TCU in light of the past three years. However, those he worked directly for and with were great.

He learned that Jim Garner struggled hard to secure this job for him. Jim found TCU's abdication of its role in Kent's life rotten and pressured the athletic director to create a new position. Now, Kent couldn't wait to start announcing football games. He made the cubby-hole of an office his own, complete with notes pasted to the wall. His four favorites:

- A foot must give up the security of one rung of a ladder before it can gain the security and achievement of a higher rung.

- The difficult we do today; the impossible takes a little longer.

- All learning is the process of remembering the past and applying the lessons you learned from it.

112

- The measure of a man's evolution is his acceptance of the unacceptable.

Communications with the State Department and Russia continued, slowly, but negotiations progressed. The trip was just a matter of time. His family finally settled onto an even keel as well. Relations bettered between Al and Denise, though his mother was pretty tired of late. With getting everyone up and dressed each morning, going to work, returning home to the usual routine after Al picked up Kent, Denise's hands stayed full. But everyone's spirits were high. They all had a change in attitude, though Kent could not pinpoint exactly why. The idea of perception being reality, however, kept dancing through his mind.

In August Carole and Larry moved to Grand Prairie to be closer to the family. Al found Larry a teaching job. Kent reveled in playing with his three-month-old niece, Dana. Shoot, Dana had been over a month old before Kent and Al ever laid eyes on her. But now, with Carole and Larry living close by, they saw her all the time. A baby can sure bring joy into your life, Kent thought. Would he ever have one of his own?

Terry Lynn and Brad still lived in Houston, but often traveled up to Grand Prairie. The person missing from the picture was Terry Stanford, who visited only once all summer. That great new quarterback must've swept her off her feet, Kent muttered.

But all in all, things were better. The fall of '77 brought a fuller life than he had experienced in a long time. Throughout the holidays and into 1978, real advances came concerning the Russia trip. He knew one thing — this year he would go.

Kent remained constantly in the press. So did America's medical community. One long feature story about his struggle toward Leningrad quoted Dr. Carter from T.I.R.R. as saying, "I don't want to hurt Kent but...the Russians have absolutely *nothing* to offer, and, in fact, might be a decade *behind* the U.S." The controversy would almost be comical if so much weren't at stake.

At his desk, reading yet another account of his Russia quest and another authority's response, Kent said to no one and to everyone, "But what is at stake is life."

✧

113

Denise sat and stared at TCU's gymnasium walls, oblivious to the roars and pandemonium surrounding her. She had no idea which basketball team led the game but was proud to hear her son's voice over the P.A. Kent did a good job announcing. And he loved it.

She spoke with no one during these games. Though being around the kids and the school did wonders for Kent's morale — and she *was* grateful for that — TCU's betrayal still gnawed on her nerves. Damn them. She and Al kept monetary concerns from Kent as best they could, but the reality remained that they labored to get by. They labored hard. Sometimes in the night she lay awake and worried if indeed they could ever make it. But they would. They must.

Her stomach ached, as it often did at these games. And then Kent's booming voice echoed across the speakers announcing TCU's win. She saw the huge smile on his face, and all was forgotten for a time, as her son relished a victory that was as much his as the team's. Then she and Al rose and started the arduous process of maneuvering Kent out of the coliseum, into the van and home.

Her stomachaches increased, leaving a rancid taste in her mouth whenever her feet stood on TCU soil. Finally Denise quit going at all. Al and Kent traveled to the games without her.

What a relief, she thought, watching them drive away. Exhausted, Denise collapsed onto the couch. But it was a good tired — the result of having toiled hard and made a step forward. The trip to Polenov finally looked possible, this year perhaps. That ray of hope worked wonders on Kent's attitude. Coupled with his job success and the friendship of Jim Garner and others in Sports Information, her boy was happy again. No price could be placed upon that.

She and Al were also back on track. Never, ever, let anyone say paralysis happens only to an individual. Its effects run crazily through the entire network of family in such unforeseen and odd ways.

For the longest time, she could not be intimate with Al. Whether this was due to exhaustion and stress or the horror of her son's loss of physical sensation, Denise could not be certain. But with time and faith and hope, they sorted that out. Now Denise dozed on the couch, drifting into soft-focus dreams of seeing her son standing.

A few weeks later, Kent passed his driver's license test. As he drove away for the first time by himself, a tightness crept up Denise's legs.

Of course he'd call when he got to work, he promised. She stood rapping her fingers on the phone, waiting for it to ring. Finally, it did. No problem.

Throughout that spring, Denise awaited the ringing phone and her son's voice assuring her he arrived safely wherever he went. And though she felt terror each time he drove off, she concealed the emotion. Kent was so happy to have this one freedom. Al fixed up the new van with a C.B. radio in case of emergency, easing that worry.

The ability to drive created a new world for her son. Having some measure of independence caused his quick wit and jovial attitude to return in full force. His temper never waned though, especially since Denise's hair styling skills didn't develop to Kent's satisfaction. Only Terry Stanford possessed that touch, and she had disappeared from the scene.

Kent pushed Terry to date until eventually she fell for someone. This past year, they saw little of her. With his new-found freedom, Kent now dated another too.

The "little English girl," Denise called her. Kent snapped at this description, but for the life of her, Denise couldn't remember the girl's name. Marla or Marsha or the like. She was sweet enough, in a childlike sort of way. She looked *maybe* sixteen, though Kent angrily swore she was nineteen. A trivial difference, Denise replied, as Kent was twenty-four. But she knew what her son was doing and whom he was trying to forget.

As the summer of '78 wore on, the Russia arrangements dragged as well. All signs still pointed to go, though *when* the trip might happen remained anybody's guess. The family, however, settled into a routine, and for the first time in years, Denise Waldrep felt some peace.

Kent sweated at his desk as he charted stat sheets for incoming freshmen football players. The sweltering August heat infiltrated even the air-conditioned buildings, leaving no place safe from the searing temperatures.

The phone rang. Impatiently Kent answered, not wanting to lose his place. On the line was Jim Wright's personal secretary.

"Kent, the Congressman wanted to call you himself, but he's been

115

tied up in meetings all morning and doesn't look to get out soon," she began, her voice wavering. "So he asked me to call. Are you sitting down?"

"That's been my habit lately," he joked.

She laughed, an electrical tinge to the sound. Then she began breathlessly. "Well, guess what? The trip to Russia has been approved for October! Of course, we'll help with the visas, passports and..." she listed details that Kent couldn't catch. Her voice continued a while before saying goodbye.

Kent inhaled deeply before dialing his mom and dad.

"Mom?"

"Hi, honey. What's going on?"

"Mom, it's, um, it's..."

"Kent, are you okay? Has there been an accident?"

"Mom..."

Jim Garner, his secretary, and TCU's basketball coach stood listening by the door. Jim stepped into the room and took the receiver from Kent's hand. As Kent cried, Jim told Denise that the Russia trip was a go. Kent would be admitted to the Polenov Institute in October. For the rest of the day his office was filled with laughter and tears. The prayers of so many friends had been answered.

Over the next two months, the public outpouring amazed everyone. Of course, the press jumped on the story, and Kent again became front-page news across the country. American neurologists and neurosurgeons maligned the Russian approach. Their criticism was simultaneously overt and subtle. And, of course, their credentials were impeccable.

Dr. Murray Goldstein, Deputy Director for the Neurological Sciences and Disorders for the National Institute of Neurological and Communicative Disorders and Stroke, summed up the professional view, in a story that ran nation-wide.

"If you were in a wheelchair," Dr. Goldstein said, "the only objective you would have would be to get out and you would seize any straw. I think the Russians are being misinterpreted by people who are desperate for a straw. The hard fact of the matter is that they've got to live with the truth."

Kent fumed. Did the entire world think he was nuts? Did *everyone*

116

believe he grasped at elusive straws? What about Bob Hurt, the race car driver paralyzed in an accident, who traveled to the Institute for treatment and now could stand? What about him?

When Kent was six he'd gotten a dachshund. For twelve years he dearly loved Fritz. Not long before Kent's departure to TCU, Fritz started limping. A tumor had developed in his hind leg, and though the vet tried to shrink it, nothing worked. One day, Fritz completely went down. He became paralyzed. Kent rushed him to the vet. The vet prescribed putting the beloved dog to sleep, saying Fritz would get progressively worse and go through much more pain. There's nothing we can do, the vet said.

So Kent did it. He held his best childhood friend while the vet gave Fritz a shot.

There's nothing more we can do. Though this diagnosis had probably been correct, Kent often wondered why he gave in so easily. Now the incident reminded him of the AMA's response to paralysis in people — shove them under the rug and pretend their problems don't exist. There is no cure. *There's nothing we can do.* The professional position on paralysis wasn't exactly euthanasia, but it was close.

Again, Kent found himself fighting the establishment. And again, he refused to quit till the fat lady sang. No one would tell him a cure was impossible. No one lived in this body but him. And *no* one would steal his hope.

Not only was public interest piqued, but society's support flooded in as well. Along with all the publicity and fascination being generated, TCU jumped into the act, too. Frank Windegger and the athletic department began a fund-raising drive to help send the Waldreps to Russia. Although the treatments were free under the Soviet health care system, the flight and expenses for Al and Denise's stay had to be paid out of pocket. Whether TCU got involved because of all the media hype and pressure (not to mention that the publicity aided the university's image) was beside the point. The family desperately needed the funds. Besides, so many caring, sincere folks were involved in the effort that for the time all transgressions were forgotten. TCU ultimately raised ten thousand sorely needed dollars.

A Grand Prairie fund was established as well. Kurt Waggoner, a long-time family friend, sponsored a benefit dinner as Kent's departure date neared. Waggoner footed the entire dinner bill himself, so that all donations went to Kent. The lavish black-tie event attracted an enormous crowd.

The night of the benefit, Kent couldn't wait to get there. Marti, the "little English girl," went with him, which, of course, infuriated Denise. His mother wanted him to take Terry Stanford. Well, Terry could just go with her fabulous quarterback. See if he cared.

Terry Stanford entered the Wood Crest Country Club amid a host of others attending the Kent Waldrep Fund Raising Dinner. In her black satin cocktail dress, she knew she looked good. All the men gave her the once-over. Wonder what Kent would think?

Immediately she found Carole, then Terry Lynn, and finally Denise. Denise hugged her as if Terry had risen from the dead.

Lots of folks she hadn't seen in a long while greeted her during the evening. Everyone seemed glad to see her. Everyone except Kent, who stayed coolly distant. Okay, she deserved that.

Marti sat with the family rather than with Kent at the head table. Denise was right; the girl looked sixteen. Okay, Terry consented again, I deserve this, too.

The ballroom hushed as Kent rolled toward the podium to speak. He began by thanking, over and again, all those who supported him from the beginning and continued to now. He spoke of the hope fostered by the Russian therapy and how wonderful this chance was.

How handsome he looked in his tux, how self-assured and confident. How happy. What a difference from the scared boy Terry returned to that first spring of '75. How much he had grown in these three and a half years. And now came the chance to be whole again.

"Last but not least," Kent continued, "I'd like to thank the person who's done the most for me, who's stood by me and helped me the most through these trying times."

Blood raced through Terry's veins. Her heartbeat quickened as adrenaline pumped through her body. With palms flat on the table she pushed her feet up under the chair in order to rise more easily.

"Marti," Kent said, "would you please stand up?"

Applause as Marti stood and Kent finished his speech drummed the life from whatever was left of Terry's heart. She stumbled from the table. Through hot tears, she struggled into the bathroom, leaned against the luxuriously upholstered dressing area, and wept. Then Denise was there and Terry Lynn and they comforted and held her, but it wasn't enough, would never be enough, and Terry knew that Kent meant this to be the final blow. He probably never loved her anyway, no matter what Denise said, but rather had merely needed her. And when she wouldn't let him depend solely on her, he found someone who would.

Terry left soon after that, heart heavy and with nowhere to turn. But on October 17, 1978, she drove to DFW International Airport, unable to keep away from Kent's departure for Leningrad.

He almost didn't go however. The Polenov Institute failed to update the Soviet Ministry of Health on Kent's schedule, and the Waldreps waited till that very day for the green-light call.

"Thank you for coming," Denise whispered, hugging her. "I know this was hard for you."

"I couldn't *not* come."

Through hordes of well-wishers and a flood of media, Terry waded forward to wish Kent luck. Though he looked ready to fly without a plane, his eyes filled for a second when he saw her.

And in those sleepy, hazel eyes, Terry saw the Kent she knew, saw all the promise and hope that had survived so much already and the courage that would sustain him. She hugged him quickly before the media converged.

Then Kent, Denise, and Al boarded the plane bound first for London, then Leningrad. As it taxied away, Terry stood watching through the windows, Terry Lynn on one side, Carole on the other. They watched until the jet roared skyward, carrying the wishes and dreams of untold numbers of people with it, and those of the trio by the window as well. The three women looked at one another, a silent prayer passing between them. It was the continuation of a prayer each had prayed for four years now. And it was one that Terry Stanford would keep constantly on her lips as the man she still loved moved tenaciously toward hope.

119

✧ CHAPTER EIGHT ✧

TO RUSSIA WITH HOPE

Kent stared through the window of the Braniff 747 into darkness. He'd finished supper and settled into his seat, waiting for *Smokey and the Bandit* to light up the screen.

As had the first few weeks following his injury, this whole day seemed like a dream. So much press. So many relatives and friends to see him off. Bear Bryant called as the family packed to leave. That gruff voice bid them an enthusiastic bon voyage, thrilled at Kent's newest quest to beat the odds.

The leaving proved more difficult than Kent imagined, though it couldn't compare with his great expectations.

That he carried the same expectations from so many gave him added purpose and strength.

No matter what happened in Russia, the trip was already a success. Merely to make the public aware of the U.S. doctors' hopeless attitude toward paralysis, while emphasizing the need for more research, signaled a touchdown. It wasn't the Super Bowl but more like a wildcard spot in the playoffs. But his willingness to try alternative approaches — both for his own personal progress and the gain of others — at least initiated debate.

In the air, he wrote this first journal entry:

> *I feel very strongly about my crusade for a positive attitude toward spinal cord injuries. For the medical profession to profess a knowledge of how it feels to be paralyzed and cope with life is as absurd as me arguing medical terminology with them. No matter how many years they deal with paralyzing injuries, they can never relate to what's going on inside a patient's mind. I feel that given an honest but positive approach from the beginning most cord-injured people could deal with*

120

life much quicker and with more incentive. Each individual must be provided the tools and materials to build his own attitude.

Kent put down his pen as the lights dimmed and the movie started. When it finished most folks slept, but his eyes never closed. What would the treatments be like? What if the doctors were as negative as those he knew? How would the Russian people respond to an American? Would any of this hurt?

These were not new questions, but they circled through his mind this night. When the plane landed in Great Britain, Kent still hadn't slept.

They spent two days in London, sightseeing, resting, and then flew through Copenhagen to Leningrad on Saturday night. An AP reporter left a message at the Leningrad Hotel, and Kent spoke with her briefly. She also left him some Russian candy, laughing that it would be the best food he ate while there. Wonder what that meant?

The rooms were small, the bathrooms, tiny. Plumbing fixtures from the 1950s adorned them. The beds stood one foot off the floor but felt comfortable. All lights shone very dimly. Their first Russian meal — beef steak, sauce, carrots, potatoes, and green beans — tasted as if boiled together in one pot.

As they returned to the room Kent asked, "How about some of that candy?"

Al kept his ear to the phone, trying to run down the consulate in Leningrad. No answer.

Nor was there the next day. Finally, Al learned the number had changed. He easily reached the consulate after that. The Polenov Institute awaited their arrival.

All of Sunday, Kent's stomach was tied in knots. What to expect? On the plane from Copenhagen, a stewardess asked if he came for *The* treatment. When he said yes, she told him of its great benefits. And, that he would get better.

On Monday morning, Kent checked into the Polenov Institute. All the way there snow fell. Temperatures hovered in the thirties. Two employees of the consul-general's office translated English to Russian and back again. One of them, Nona, would be their translator for the duration.

The hulking green dinosaur of a hospital greeted the Waldreps. Four stories high, with massive gray-white columns and arches and smallish windows, it appeared the world's grimmest building. Kent tensed, and his mother's mouth set into a straight line.

Inside, however, all the doctors and nurses were quite friendly and helpful.

Kent surveyed his surroundings. The hospital was ancient. On the way to his room, he watched the dingy hospital interior pass by, with all its outdated equipment. No heat filled the corridors. An antique bed, hard as a brick, awaited him. He was alone in the room, though the others were full. This hospital looked straight out of 1950s America. What the hell did I get myself into now?

A nurse wheeled him into an examining room, where four doctors, including Dr. Ugryumov, the director of the Institute, and Dr. Zotov, the chief of neurosurgery, checked for feeling, rubbed matchsticks across his stomach, scrutinized arm and eye movements.

Then everyone sat in a circle while the doctors explained, with interpretive help from Nona, what they planned to do.

For the first two to three weeks, they would run tests. Then they'd decide whether to operate, and what course of treatment to pursue.

"They are very impressed," Nona said, "with your abilities so far. Every one," she paused, nodding at each smiling face, "wants to help you if at all possible."

All the doctors shook his and Al's hands, placing palms on Kent's shoulders. What a difference from those cold, immovable faces at home.

Dinner at the hospital was similar to that at the hotel — boiled meat and potatoes and vegetables. Bad to fair, Kent thought, closing his eyes. He drifted to sleep, wondering what the next few weeks would bring.

What the first week brought was pretty awful food and many more tests. How could these folks live on this terrible boiled everything? They performed blood tests and an electroencephalogram. Therapy began as well. The doctors stopped by all the time, always kind and friendly and willing to talk. Of course, unless Nona accompanied them, the Waldreps had difficulty knowing what the doctors said. But an almost immediate interchange of English/Russian began, and before long, Kent, Denise, and Al understood enough Russian to get by.

X-rays were taken of his neck and chest. Therapy started with weightlifting to strengthen his stomach — part of the process of learning to stand. The doctor quoted from Edgar Allan Poe as he explained the procedure. Poe was the doctor's favorite poet.

After a supper of Russian stew (mutton, carrots, and potatoes), bread, butter, and hot tea — the best meal yet in Russia — Kent settled in to write in his journal:

> *I should sleep well tonight, am tired. Big enlightenment — attitude of Russian doctors. Not negative, always positive about helping. Show such willingness to treat each one individually. Hospital comfort was better in the '40s in the U.S., but once I get used to feeling grubby I'll make it. I'm fickle about clean hair and clean body. It's so cold in the hospital the doctors won't let me wash my hair — so I'm not shaving either. Completely grubbed out! Doctors attitude refreshing. Attitude in treating patients so much better. Don't speak of giving up hope. Doctor very warm hearted and involved — typical Russian loves Americans. Everyone friendly.*

Kent put down his pen and laughed, remembering the view during X-ray — a ceiling stained from water leaks. Some building inspector would have a mouth-foaming fit at finding that back home.

More tests were taken that week, and new therapy begun. One of the doctors taught Kent exercises for thinking movement to his fingers. He liked her and loved her attitude.

"I will work with you every day," she said, examining him in his underwear. "You have sportsman's body." They laughed.

His therapist, Helen, proved to be an absolute slave driver, which he loved. Her favorite saying amounted to, "Must build stronger body to walk." Whenever he began to flag, she said either that or, "Boy must be strong," with a frown on her face. Kent dared not cross her.

He wondered what people at home would think and wrote in his journal:

> *I hope friends and those concerned aren't disappointed if I show no improvement, but I'm not at all depressed at this point. Am getting used*

to the people, routine, and customs. Even washed and dried my hair this morning (beat the system). Sometimes when I'm uncomfortable I get a sinking feeling about being so far from home. Last night I tried to explain I was hot to a nurse with hand motions (fanning). She left and came back with a basin for washing me.

He continued to try to choke down unrecognizable food. And though the staff cooked up things he might like, he started losing weight. Denise and Al brought him restaurant fare to supplement his diet, but not often enough.

His doctors often stopped in, sometimes just for language lessons — both ways. They all laughed a lot.

In bed one night, Kent realized the injury had happened four years ago that very day. Four years. In the journal he wrote:

I really thought 3 years ago that I would be walking by now. I didn't know enough then to put this into proper perspective.

I know I will walk again someday, but now I also know I can survive and contribute like I am. I also know more about myself and what I need. Giving others the hope of improvement and eventual cure is a message that needs to be spread. Also more dignity and opportunities need to be fought for.

I feel good about what I've accomplished in the last four years both physically and socially. Let's hope the next four years are even more productive.

Death hadn't taken him, he thought lying in the darkness, nor had the American system. Now if he could just live through this Russian cuisine.

Tomorrow he would have another myelogram. Thank God these doctors performed their own tests. And though their facilities belonged to the Stone Age, they accomplished so very much with so little. Helen could work miracles with modern equipment. The entire staff geared itself to getting the most progress out of each patient. What a switch.

I'm finally used to the routine, he thought. I'm encouraged by the staff's willingness and humanity. Kent reached to add one more note in the journal:

I'm becoming more sure I've done the right thing. Awfully homesick though (hungry for junk food too).

Now, if only McDonald's would deliver...

Denise bathed Kent's face with cold towels all Friday night. He slept for fifteen-minute intervals. His head ached terribly from the myelogram. Instead of dye, the doctors injected oxygen into the spinal layers, which knocked Kent for a loop. But this test would determine whether or not surgery was needed.

Al got lost in the subway system the next morning, but arrived by 8:00 a.m. They coaxed Kent into eating a bite and poured juice down him. Throughout Saturday, they watched a war rage in his head. The doctors said the oxygen must find a way out of his body, and it moved finally from his head to his stomach. On Sunday, the volcano erupted. But since he had consumed nothing since Thursday night, not much emerged. By evening, he started to feel better.

They would find out soon which road the treatments would take. Not soon enough, Denise thought. Then everyone would rest easier. Kent had been in a bad mood, with the tests and indecision. Between not eating for three days and the terrible food, he lost a good bit of weight.

"This is damned ridiculous," Al said a few days later. "Kent's gonna starve to death eating this stuff. Hell, I'm gonna starve to death."

Denise patted her hips. "Wouldn't hurt me to lose a few."

Al grinned at her and winked. "Nah," he said, "don't you lose any either. But I'm gonna do something about getting weight back *on* Kent."

Denise watched him disappear into the cold. If she knew Al, he *would* do something. But what? In this land where they couldn't even order supper without Nona? Boy, some English conversation sounded good about now, and an order of french fries...

Finally, on November 1, they met with the doctors to decide what to do.

"Dr. Ugryumov says surgery is not necessary," Nona interpreted. "The tests show no pressure on the cord. The cord is injured from only the front and in good shape in back."

Thank God, Denise thought.

Al rubbed his palm through his hair and said, "But the American doctors told us the cord had degenerated."

Nona translated and all the doctors shook their heads.

"No," she stated. "This is not true. The cord is in good shape."

Al shook his head. "American medicine strikes again," he said.

"The therapy," Nona continued, "will be intense, positive rehabilitation, including enzyme injections, hyperbaric oxygen treatments, physical therapy, and massage. Dr. Ugryumov is very positive about recovering more function with increased therapy. Estimated time of stay, one month."

Denise looked to Al and an expression passed between them. What we prayed for, Al's gaze said, no surgery.

Kent immediately started exchanging translations with one of the nurses, and Denise and Al left with Nona for "Sarka," reportedly the best restaurant in town.

The meal was marvelous — steak with mushrooms and tomato salad. Finally, decent food! They ordered and delivered some to Kent, who ate every bite and then traveled on to the consul-general's office to pick up groceries on order. "I'll start cooking tomorrow," Al said.

Before closing tired eyes that night, Denise wrote in her journal:

> *Kent is in a much better frame of mind since he knows what they are going to do. Al will start cooking tomorrow and we will put Kent's weight back on him. Everyone is relieved with a definite decision made. This will be about a three-week treatment and then another meeting will take place and we will see from there. I look to be home by the middle of December. We are very positive about the treatment. With God's help we will make it.*

The next day, Al stood over a makeshift stove, cooking. "How about some of the best french fries this side of the Atlantic," he said, spooning a bunch of sizzling potatoes onto a plate, squeezing a dollop of ketchup beside them and handing it all to his son. Kent ate like a refugee survivor. "Just an hors d'oeuvre," Al said, winking at him. Turning to the stove and twirling his metal spoon, Al cooked steak and squash to go along with the fries, and Kent responded as if he'd died and gone to heaven. Just the salty aroma of grease and potatoes sent Denise to paradise.

"I talked to Brad and Terry Lynn earlier," she said, savoring a fry. "Everything's okay at home."

Kent brightened. "Did you tell them what's happening?" he asked.

Denise nodded and then laughed. "But not for long. That call cost a fortune."

"I can't wait to start," Kent stated, chewing his fries. "We did the right thing, coming here."

Yes, Denise thought.

Al nodded, saying, "And three to four weeks of this stuff oughta fatten you like a calf headed to market." He finished cooking and ladled it all onto a big plate. "Here you go. Eat till it kills you."

They watched until Kent ate every bite. For a time they visited and then put him to bed and left for the hotel. These first few weeks had been long, but Denise kicked her homesickness under the bed and lay down, asleep as soon as she felt the pillow.

The next day, therapy began in earnest. Enzyme shots were injected into his hip and leg, and electrolysis applied to his neck. A therapist made a plaster of Paris cast of Kent's legs for his standing program. His weight workout continued, and he began massage therapy.

At 10:00 p.m. the next night, Denise wrote pages in her journal. She paused and then began:

> *Al and I cooked steak fingers and french fries and we all had a feast. Kent ate and ate. Good to see him eating again. Kent and I played gin as Al went to Consul-General's to get mail, cokes, potato chips and peanuts. Sure did taste good. Got another letter from Dad and Kent got 2. Got football scores which made him smile.*
>
> *Nona came over about 11:00 and it's always so good to see her as we find out everything when she arrives. We ask questions and she checks with the doctor and tells us what they are doing.*
>
> *It's always good to get back to the hotel and relax as 12 to 13 hours a day at the clinic is very tiring.*

127

Closing her eyes, Denise knew that though he never said it, her son felt as homesick as she did. Well, that was to be expected. At least with Al cooking, they wouldn't wither from starvation. Al often played pool with U.S. marines at the consulate, winning groceries from them. Denise and Kent ribbed him constantly about keeping his pool game sharp. They were only partially kidding.

Many press people called the consulate to check on Kent, including CBS and Nikki Finke from AP. The hospital administrator nixed letting the calls come into the hospital as that caused too much confusion, so they were routed through the hotel. Al kept everyone abreast of Kent's progress. The doctor brought in a cameraman who took photos of Kent, and some of Kent and the doctor for UP.

For the next five days, Leningrad shut down to celebrate the anniversary of the Russian Revolution. The battleship from which the troops had embarked to storm the czar's house was anchored on the Neva outside Al and Denise's window.

Some therapy continued, but not much. The trio spent a lot of time playing gin. John Carlson, from the consulate-general's office, invited Denise and Al over for dinner one night.

"How nice it was to speak English," Denise said as she and Al walked through the cold into the hospital.

Al drew his arm around her shoulders and hugged her close. They found Kent playing gin with several other patients. He played badly — down many rubles — but the sound of his laughter comforted her. And now that he found friends his own age, they left him for longer periods. The kids communicated through hand signals, facial expressions, Kent's smidgen of Russian, and their bits of English. Though comical looking, it worked.

Back at the hotel, Al rustled up a bottle of champagne, some bread, and a bowlful of caviar from the hotel bar. They never knew when either establishment would be open; no one abided by posted business hours.

While he was gone, Denise wrote:

Kent's mood is okay but getting very homesick and hungry for good food, as we all are. Almost three weeks that we have been in Leningrad. Long time from home. Really miss family and friends. It's hard

128

to try to stay happy and in a good mood when you are lonely. We must try harder.

Al presented a feast, and Denise savored the luscious caviar. Russian food may be terrible, but the caviar was divine, as were many of the hearty breads and pastries.

Al sat beside her, pouring champagne. Outside, the sky illuminated with showers of red, green, and yellow lights — a fireworks display of epic proportions. This celebration rivaled America's Christmas.

They looked upon a beautiful view of the Neva River and the fireworks bursting above it. In their cramped, primitive room, Denise experienced the beauty of Leningrad. Where else could one dine regularly on champagne and caviar? Watch a city celebrate for five days with fireworks and parades? Where else could her husband win peanut butter, soup, V-8 juice, peanuts, canned beef Stroganoff, and creamed corn by beating the pants off Marines at pool? Or take her to a bad Doris Day movie on Wednesday nights at the consul-general's? Of course, the subway system had pretty much baffled Al, but he managed.

Al took her hand in his. So long ago she had fallen in love with this handsome man. They had sailed over many rough seas. But always, he stood right beside her, coming through in the hard times, even if that meant serving her champagne and caviar in a foreign world.

She kissed his cheek, and in silence they nibbled, sipped their delicacies, watched the show outside, and held tightly to one another.

Finally, the holiday ended on Thursday, November 9, and the routine began again. Al fixed breakfast about 8:00 a.m. Denise washed and dried Kent's hair. Then Dr. Ugryumov dropped in.

Rubbing one palm over his nearly bald head, the doctor said in his deep, booming voice, "Hyperbaric oxygen treatments today."

"Utro?" Kent asked.

Ugryumov laughed heartily enough for his portly belly to shake. "Yes," he said, "this morning."

The treatment lasted about forty-five minutes, and other than

129

the feel of his ears popping, Kent experienced no side effects. The technician unloaded him from the round, torpedo-shaped tube.

"First used by Russian cosmonauts," the smiling young man said, helping Kent back into his chair.

"What about submarine commanders?" Kent asked, and the technician laughed.

From there he went to massage therapy, then lunch, then physical therapy in the afternoon. Al cooked steak fingers for supper, and Kent ate every morsel.

"Here, look at this," Denise said, handing a letter to him.

It came from a U.S. couple with an injured son. They became interested in the treatments after reading of Kent's pilgrimage. Apparently, he was still big news at home.

"I suspect there will be more of those," Denise said, staring at the envelope.

Al rubbed clean the frying pan and said, "Just wait'll we get back home."

Kent scanned the pages, and then looked up. "There oughta be a central way to answer people," he began. "A way to get information out, since our neurologists won't cooperate."

Denise patted his arm, rising to leave. "Let's worry about that when we *get* home," she said, kissing his forehead. "Besides, tomorrow's the big day."

Kent watched his parents leave and then stared up at the ceiling. Yes, tomorrow would be a very big day.

The next morning, Friday, November 10, 1978, Kent awakened at 9:30 a.m. Denise washed and dried his hair. He received a massage, and then spent an hour and a half in the oxygen chamber, where he mentally worked on finger exercises. When he returned from the chamber, the physical therapists were waiting.

First they attached the special leg braces, then lace-up boots. Next to his bed stood a large rounded walker.

With little fanfare and not much talk, they stood him in it. My *God*, how different the room appeared! Faces seemed different as he looked them in the eye. After four years of being four feet tall, how strange it was to look *down* on people.

With the therapists pulling ropes attached to Kent's legs, he walked.

Only a few steps, a few slow, difficult steps. But he was walking! For a mere five minutes did he stand upright and move forward, but those were five precious minutes. Dizziness almost defeated him, but he willed himself to stay up. The strain on his shoulders and arms, more severe than anything since the injury, felt as if the weight of the world bore down upon them. But man, what a rush!

Those awkward first steps lacked any semblance of coordination, but the euphoria of having weight on his feet overcame that as well. *My Lord,* he thought, *I feel whole again.*

By the time they unhooked him from the metal frame, his arms and shoulders shook from exertion.

He finished the afternoon with enzyme shots and more physical therapy for his hands.

As the days passed, his regimes progressed. He walked longer with each session. Almost all of his time during the day consisted of some therapy or another, sometimes not even pausing for lunch, so that by evening, exhaustion engulfed him. All the exercise coupled with poor nutrition caused an energy drain, although Al fixed real food whenever possible. But midway into his stay, Kent found himself fighting — both physically and mentally.

He wrote:

> *Doctor Zotov came by to visit and while talking mentioned the fact that this treatment might take 1 or 2 years. Wanted to reassure us.*
>
> *I have no energy. It's kind of frustrating to do all this work and see no results. But I have to remember how slowly the nerves heal. I hope others aren't disappointed if I return with no new movements. Must get positive feelings across to them.*
>
> *Walked furthest distance yet in walker.*

He tried keeping the fears to himself as Denise and Al had their own weariness to deal with, but his mom could tell. His moods weren't the best in the world. And though she took his tirades in stride, she came down hard at times too. Only Terry Stanford could scold him as well. Of course, *she* hadn't written. But then, Terry never was one to write much. He sure did miss her. Oh, and Marti, too.

A reporter and photographer from the *Chicago Tribune* came by for

131

an interview. It was fun talking with the media again. They asked a lot about the walker.

"Yeah," he answered one question, "the world definitely looks a lot different when you're standing up. You get a different view of life."

He paused and then continued, "Before, I can remember my main thought on seeing somebody like this was strictly pity. I would really feel sorry about the guy and wonder, how does he cope? I knew I couldn't deal with it.

"A wheelchair brings you a completely different perspective — you've *got* to deal with it. You either deal with it, or you just waste away."

The reporter jotted quickly while the photographer snapped away. Then he turned to Denise and asked, "What was it like for you, Mrs. Waldrep, to see your son standing?"

Denise tilted her head. For a minute, she hesitated in uncharacteristic silence. Her eyes grew moist. Then softly she said, "After four years, I had forgotten how tall he was."

They talked of the Russian approach versus the American one. Kent explained the various therapies. They seemed impressed with his progress and promised to send copies of the article.

I hope they report it truthfully, he thought. No, I'm not skipping yet but the work in the walker really gets my heart pumping. The Russians maintained that you must retrain muscles in order to walk once the nerves heal. Made sense to him. No physical therapy yet came close to enhancing strength as did the walker.

Finally, the workouts became easier as his body adjusted. He walked now for an hour. Al kept winning at the pool table (though still getting lost on the subway), and Kent's appetite and diet improved. His energy returned full-force.

He also made a host of friends, and in the evenings, Alexander, Victor, Rafael, Boris, and Lucha came to visit, toting their dictionaries. He let them listen to his tapes, and they grew to love American music. They played lots of gin and Kent continued to lose many rubles, not that he cared much.

And he met Alla.

She arrived one evening with Lucha to learn American words.

"Alla," Kent said the name back to her.

She smiled, causing her brown eyes to dance in her small face framed by auburn hair. Alla wore no makeup, and her natural beauty needed none.

At first they struggled to communicate, as did everyone, but soon learned enough to speak and write their expressions. Most evenings, Alla came to visit, and they laughed until the nurses chased everybody to bed. They spoke of politics and culture, of boys and girls. Alla said there was no God, that He was an impostor. And, both Alla and Lucha also identified Nixon as a good man. How different their lives were from Kent's.

On the night after American doctors visited the hospital, Kent put into his journal:

> *Went to Ugryumov's office after oxygen treatment to meet with 3 visiting doctors from U.S. One is with the V.A. spinal cord in Washington D.C.*
>
> *Explained to them my program here; didn't ask me many questions; appeared skeptical and disinterested. In a one or two hour visit they cannot learn much about the Soviets' positive approach; I mentioned Roger Frank and the V.A. guy immediately disclaimed the fact he got significant improvement. Typical reaction.*
>
> *Walked over an hour today and it's getting smoother; really strengthening shoulders, stomach and back; legs getting firmer.*

The routine continued to become easier and more enjoyable. His strength grew by the day. The walking therapy proved positive both mentally and physically. He finally gained some weight due to his dad's pool winnings. Al also purchased supplies from Finland through the consulate, and Kent's stamina multiplied. But the Russian subway system kept outfoxing Al.

One day Alla informed him she could no longer visit in his room. Neither could the rest of the young Russians. When Denise and Al inquired about this, the nurses replied that they thought the others bothered Kent and the staff wanted him completely comfortable. Through Nona, they explained that Kent enjoyed the company, and visitation rights were restored.

Before sleeping that night, Kent wrote:

Spent all day with Alla. Played Russian cards; she cheated me! I cheated her playing poker. She curled her hair today — looked American — and massaged my hands. Learned Russian song, 4 verses; impressed doctors.

No letters from Marti or Terry yet. Tends to make me think something is bothering Marti. Terry never takes time to write.

Have made date with Alla for Moscow Olympics and Black Sea holiday (if I'm walking). She loves me anyway. She understands cause she's studying to be a doctor. Knows about my injury. Fantastic girl.

✧ CHAPTER NINE ✧

THE MORE WE SEEM DIFFERENT, THE MORE WE ARE THE SAME

On the night before Thanksgiving, Denise sat looking at the Neva River and writing in her journal:

> *A man from Tass came to take pictures of Kent on the walker and in the oxygen chamber. We hope to buy some of them from him if possible.*
>
> *ABC just called and they want to see Kent so maybe they will come this Sunday. CBS also wants to come. Sunday is the only day they can get in to see Kent.*
>
> *Got letter from Terry Lynn and Dad today. Love our mail. Really looking forward to going home. Very homesick!*

She and Al had just returned from their Wednesday night movie at the marine base, and was it ever cold coming home. Minus thirteen as they waited outside thirty minutes for a taxi. But you dressed for it here, and the weather didn't daunt them. Except, perhaps, that darkness prevailed by three in the afternoon.

The next day, they celebrated Thanksgiving at John and Lucy Carlson's. The children made place-cards for the table with turkeys and Indians and pilgrims; then Lucy played the piano, and everyone joined in a Thanksgiving hymn.

The turkey and dressing, cranberries and salad tasted as if from heaven itself. For a time, in this American household amid the revelry of Thanksgiving, Denise felt at home.

So did Kent when a basket filled with goodies was delivered to him. Before going to bed, Denise wrote:

> *John and Lucy Carlson and their children are a wonderful family, and it's nice having people like that represent the United States. This was a*

135

good day and it helped being with friends. I will always remember this Thanksgiving Day away from home.

The next morning, Denise called Carole.

"It's fine. All's well," she told her daughter. "We leave here on the 8th, and I'll call from London and give you the rest of our arrangements."

Carole blurted, "We saw a picture of him walking. It was in the paper with a story about how the treatments are helping!"

"Yes," Denise said, trying to mask the weariness in her voice. "The walker has done a lot. Carole," she hesitated then asked, "have you talked to Terry?"

"Stanford?"

"Yes."

"Yeah, I called to tell her about him walking, but she'd already seen it in the paper. We're all so excited!"

Again Denise paused. Then she continued, "Did you ask her if she'd written?" The last time Denise spoke with Carole, she asked her daughter to phone and urge Terry to write. Kent sent numerous letters and cards, receiving no answer.

"Oh, she's just busy. You know Terry, she's not much on writing. But she was thrilled about the walking," Carole said. "And she'll be there to meet you at the airport."

They talked a bit more and hung up. Would it make any difference to Terry if Kent walked? After all this time, could Kent forgive her enough to begin again if Terry now wanted to? Would they both be better off going on with their lives apart? Was that possible, now or ever?

And though Kent reaped some progress from the treatments, they weren't dramatic. True improvements might take a year. Or more.

That weekend the temperature dropped and it started to snow. As countdown for going home began, Denise shopped for her girls — daughters who basically lost their mother in this process, daughters whom she knew still needed their mother. Especially Terry Lynn — so young and married and bound to be having all the tribulations new brides faced. Who did Terry Lynn turn to now? Could she ever forgive her mother for focusing so totally on Kent?

136

Kent's therapy remained rigorous, and he continued to improve. He walked now for over an hour. The doctors would check him one last time at the end of the week. Newspeople from Leningrad, UPI, AP, CBS, and ABC, scheduled interviews.

Thursday he received the last oxygen treatment. Two U.S. Representatives came by and talked with him. On Friday, a Soviet news crew interviewed and tried to film him, but their equipment broke down. Typical, Denise thought with a laugh.

The masseuse instructed them all that day on how to continue Kent's massages.

"You must keep up the treatments," Nona translated. "Muscles are reacting that were not doing so when we started."

Kent grinned up at Denise. He had been saying as much for a week.

That night she and Al attended *Swan Lake* at a beautiful Leningrad theater. Though some of Russia seemed so backward, the beauty of the culture took her breath away. And tomorrow there would be more filming and more packing. What to do with all the mail arriving from people seeking information about the treatment? Kent would already need a month to answer the stacks when he got home.

The next night the Marines visited, bringing the film *Can-Can* for all the patients, doctors, and nurses to watch. They laughed for two hours.

Saturday the film crew returned with better equipment, and shot an entire documentary about the family. CBS was due tomorrow, and then ABC the next day.

And Kent's fingers twitched. When he moved his hands and tried to use his fingers, they wiggled. Four years after his accident, new sensations surfaced. *All damage present three to six months after injury . . .*

Denise began mental preparations for packing, but then stopped and wrote in order to clear her mind:

Busy week ahead as it's our last week here and in one way, very sad. Glad to be going home as we miss our family very much but this has been so great for Kent that it will be sad to leave. It has given us all so much that we will miss the friends we have made and the positive approach of their work. I hope we can take all this home and help

137

others to feel it as much as we do. Kent has gathered much strength from this and I hope it shows to others.

But how to show it? True progress is sometimes so intangible. And intangibles are difficult to convey, much less prove. Well, they would deal with all that next week, when real life began again.

Kent chatted amiably with the ABC reporter. CBS's interview didn't go well the day before since Sundays at the Polenov had no routine. But today would be different.

"Has this contraption helped," the reporter, Bierbower, asked nicely enough, though Kent felt his skepticism.

"More than anything," he replied. "Well, I guess 'more than anything's' hard to say. The effects of the enzymes and oxygen treatments won't be felt for a while."

"And you've regained more feeling?"

"My stomach and back muscles have improved significantly. My hands have more feeling, and my dexterity and coordination has improved. And I have feeling in my toes."

The reporter's bushy eyebrows raised. "Really?"

Kent nodded as the therapists readied him for the walker. Bierbower busied himself with his notes until Kent was standing.

He lurched up as Kent inched forward, asking quickly, "How has this walker helped your therapy?"

Kent started to speak, and just as he did so Bierbower suddenly slumped to the floor. The nurses and doctors all rushed to him and in seconds revived the man.

As it turned out, Bierbower suffered from simple exhaustion. Boy, can I relate to that, Kent thought, chuckling inwardly. He couldn't help but laugh though — his first interview in four years standing up and the *interviewer* passed out! His luck. But bless Bierbower's heart, he had probably traveled two days straight with no rest.

Kent said softly, "We can do this later, when you're rested."

The reporter shook his head and soon stood again. "No, I'm a little jet-lag shaky, that's all. I'm ready to continue." The interview progressed. When it finished, Kent felt he had expressed the important

138

things. At least this clip should beat him home, paving the way for more press.

Kent spent the next two days saying goodbyes. On Wednesday, the doctors came for a final examination and discussion.

"Dr. Zotov stresses that the spinal cord is in excellent shape," Nona translated. "No deterioration of cord. With hard work, you should see very positive improvements." She paused a moment. "Must come back," she said, "in 1980."

They all shook hands and Kent motioned them to stay. Al and Denise gave silk roses to the nurses and pens to the doctors and staff. And Kent sang for them a Russian song he learned. Everyone cheered.

This was a good but sad day, Kent thought, lying in bed after supper. Then he thought of the newest patient, Vicki, and anger rose into his throat. He began to write:

> *Today a Colombian citizen but U.S. resident, pretty girl (Vicki, 22) checked into the hospital. Room next door.*
>
> *Vicki C-5 incomplete but no movement below shoulders (shot in the neck by would-be rapist).*
>
> *Doctors in states wouldn't perform surgery to remove bullet or myelogram to check cord.*
>
> *Went through Colombian President (uncle) to get acceptance here at Polenov.*
>
> *Person like this has more guts than any of us. She has very little incentive for living, but still manages a smile. A doctor who can stand over her bed and say no hope ever is nothing but a shell of a person. How can he predict the future of advancement in treatment. Tell her no hope and then walk out of the room.*
>
> *I admire the hell out of her and others like her.*
>
> *They're the ones with REAL COURAGE.*

Later, Alla arrived with champagne, and they talked and laughed. He invited her to supper the next night at the hotel. She frowned, saying, "I cannot come into hotel. Armed soldiers guard it." Kent promised to check into that. For a long, long while, she massaged his hands and then held him.

Kent awakened at eight the next morning. Denise washed and dried his hair, and they started saying final goodbyes to the staff.

139

"Don't cry, Olya," Kent comforted his physical therapist, "I'll be back." All morning she was with him, weeping.

As the Waldreps prepared to leave the hospital, Kent's doctors came in. They, too, were crying. They became so emotional that all left the room except Zotov, who bent and kissed his cheek and then disappeared. Hell, Kent thought, you couldn't get a tear out of a rehab doctor in America if you stuck an onion in his face.

For the first time in forty-four days, Kent saw the outside world. The consulate provided a car, and they toured the city until the sun went down.

Kent sat in the hotel suite — two bedrooms and baths and a central area with a piano — dining on champagne and caviar. Nona convinced Alla that she could come into the hotel, and Al went down to greet her. No one off the street was allowed in. As Alla predicted, armed guards stood posted at the entrances. But the door opened and in Al and Alla walked.

"Hi," Alla said, looking naturally beautiful as always. She smiled at Kent, though the light in her brown eyes looked dim.

"Champagne?"

Alla nodded.

"They're gonna miss our card games at the hospital," Kent said. "No American losing money now."

A smile graced Alla's sweet face. "And American music," she replied. "No more Olivia John." She tried to laugh but it caught, and for a moment she appeared close to tears.

"No more Olivia John," Kent echoed softly.

Nona sat nearby writing out Kent's exercises, and now and then she and Alla would confer on a word. The champagne was crisp and airy, the talk light. Kent's heart was sinking. Though he'd been homesick for so long, this goodbye would be hard.

They all went to dinner and a show downstairs, and then Alla and Kent returned to the room alone.

Sitting on the piano stool, Alla began a soft, soulful melody. Midway through it, she started to cry.

Kent said, "Come here."

"I will not stop loving you," she said in perfect English.

"Don't cry," Kent responded, tears welling in his eyes.

"I will wait for your return."

For the rest of the evening, they held each other close.

At nine-thirty the next morning, the Waldreps left for the airport. Light snow was falling. By the time they reached the terminal, the innocuous flakes evolved into a blizzard.

No one but armed guards occupied the airport. They stood lined like clothespins against the wall. Nobody spoke. An eerie silence echoed through the area. A cold silence. Dim lights washed a sepia haze over the main room as the Waldreps' bags were X-rayed though not searched. None of the guards glanced at Kent as he rolled toward the gate. Every sound of his wheels squeaked like fingernails across a blackboard.

Outside, blowing snow bit at their faces, the wind whipping gritty particles into shreds of glass. The plane sat at least five hundred yards away, encircled by an ethereal glow.

Without a word, Al started pushing Kent through the blinding snow, slowly, against the wind. For a time they seemed lost in a white sea, sliding across the ice. Finally, they reached the plane, and Kent was lifted onto it.

Only eight people rode that flight to Copenhagen. Denise's skin paled and remained colorless the entire time, while Al's mouth hardened into a crease.

Kent joked, "Well, what's one more natural disaster?" but neither parent smiled.

They arrived in London and deboarded slowly. In the airline terminal, hordes of photographers, broadcast journalists, and press of all types were gathered.

"Maybe the Royal Family's here today," Kent said, as Al pushed him toward the crowd.

"Oh!" Denise said. "We might get to see the queen!" All three Waldreps scanned the area.

"Kent!" one of the journalists called, "can you walk?"

And with that, they besieged him, popping flash bulbs and firing questions. Kent blinked, the pandemonium momentarily stunning him. *What in the name of . . . these people are here to see me!*

He answered every question, most centering upon his standing and walking. Was the therapy successful? Are you angry you couldn't receive it in the States? *Can you walk?*

Hours later, they broke away and went to the hotel where Kent ate a grilled steak, baked potato, and salad. He swore it was the best meal of his life.

An AP photographer shot rolls of Kent at London Bridge. Allan, their driver when they passed through London the first time, happily chauffeured them around again. At one point Kent picked up a peanut and put it in his mouth.

"Look," Allan said, pointing excitedly, "he couldn't do that before!"

No, Kent thought, I don't suppose I could.

The next day, he again stared out a Braniff 747 window, en route and not too far from DFW International Airport. He couldn't wait to be home and was ready to answer any and all questions.

For the last time on this trip, Kent took out his pen:

A SUCCESS OR A FAILURE?

The only way to fairly judge the merits of a trip like this is to weigh the benefits of not only my treatment and improvement but also the nationwide awareness of this problem caused by my trip, against any negative results brought by the treatment.

There were no negative results caused by my treatment.

I am not walking nor am I moving my legs, but positive improvement in strength, dexterity and coordination has resulted. I, better than anyone, know the tremendous odds I'm facing in beating paralysis. But I know only one way to live my life and quitting is not my way.

Realistically, treatment to alleviate paralysis is only now becoming a real possibility. To do something out of the ordinary or away from accepted normality usually draws criticism. The arrogance and narrow-mindedness of the neurosurgeons and personnel associated with cord injured persons has really been demonstrated with their disapproval of my treatment.

Their inability to accept a possibly positive treatment for paralytic people simply because it wasn't U.S.-initiated is characteristic of the chauvinistic attitude in the medical world.

142

There is a very real need for change in approach to treatment and rehab of persons with spinal cord injuries in the U.S. Emphasis needs to be switched from accepting the status-quo to stretching the limits of technology and medicine.

The Soviet program offers both and as of right now is the pioneering approach to this problem.

Maybe other areas of research offer a more promising and quicker method of treatment, but Soviet rehab could definitely offer more help to cord-injured people immediately.

U.S. rehab does not fulfill the potential of quadriplegic persons at this time. Strengthening at the acute stage is limited. The Soviet approach begins at acute and continues into chronic. Positive thinking is taught and hopelessness is never mentioned. The person is never subjected to totally negative vibes. A realistic and honest evaluation is made and given to the patient, in a straightforward manner. The Soviets have managed to combine professionalism, honesty and true compassion in dealing with this type of injury. They realize the need for all three. Is this an impossibility for U.S. doctors?

I will not live my life governed by limitations set by others. I feel I've initiated an approach sprinkled with positiveness and reality, with a goal of accomplishment.

Accepting life in a wheelchair will never be my fate, only a temporary stop on a journey which will not end until a cure is found. I want to add a sense of dignity and take away negativism. And, I'll make living with a disability more acceptable in all elements of our society.

I've had the opportunity not available to most. If I fail it should be worse than the failure of others. It helps me to help others.

To help others understand the problems involved with paralysis and to reprogram positive thinking into the mind of cord-injured persons is a battle that needs to be fought and has to be won.

Hope should always live in the hearts and minds of all people.

As the wheels of the jet plane touched the runway, Kent put down his pen.

Why, he wondered, had the U.S. doctors chosen paralysis as the one hopeless, incurable medical issue? Please God, help me in my battle to help others understand the need for hope in all of our lives. And to remember the suffering endured by the families.

The plane taxied to the terminal, and a peace engulfed him. God had heard his prayer, and Kent knew that HE would answer.

Yes, hope should always live in the hearts of all people.

"And with God's strength," he said softly, "we'll get it done."

Lynn and Kent returned to Birmingham in January, 1984 for Coach Paul "Bear" Bryant's funeral. Among the hundreds of former players was Joe Namath, visiting here with Kent. That's Francis Sanderson (center), another Alabama resident who adopted Kent and his family.

Then-Vice President George Bush greets Kent after swearing in Kent and his fellow members to a new term on the National Council on Disability in early 1984. It was this council that would propose the historic Americans with Disabilities Act. Kent recommended the legislation's name.

Kent and the 1985 winners of the United States Jaycees Ten Outstanding Young Men of America Award. Among those winners gathering in Tulsa, Oklahoma, in January of 1985 were 1976 Olympic champion Bruce Jenner and David Copperfield, the world-renowned master illusionist.

Former Dallas Cowboys General Manager Tex Schram hands Kent a check from NFL Charities in 1986. NFL Charities was an early supporter of Kent's foundation.

Former Dallas Cowboys and Hall of Fame Coach Tom Landry with Kent and Foundation supporter and friend Joey Nichols. Coach Landry and many Dallas Cowboys have participated in Kent's events.

Kent and best friend Terry Stanford, shown here in Kent's living room in September, 1975, and sixteen years later at the National Paralysis Foundation's Southwestern Ball in Dallas. Terry and Kent remain best friends today.

ABOVE: Kent at six months.

RIGHT: Father Al (a Robert Mitchum lookalike) and Kent at age four, ready for Easter Sunday, in 1958.

In the sixth grade, Kent threw the only no-hitter in Angleton Little League history and was also the first player never to strike out. Pictured here with the 1966 Angleton All-Star team, Kent is fourth from the left in the back row.

Football began for Kent in the fifth grade in Grand Prairie, Texas. His Longhorn football team went undefeated. (Kent's number is 20.)

LEFT: Kent really did graduate from Alvin High School. And he was a two-year honoree in the National Honor Society.

RIGHT: Kent with his oldest son, Trey, six weeks, in early 1988.

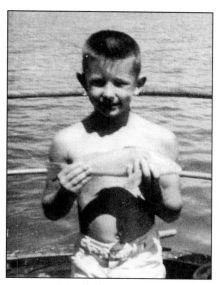

Fishing is a proud Waldrep tradition. Kent snared this prize catch in 1960 at age six, and son Trey snared his in 1994 at age six.

Kent and his beautiful wife, Lynn, at a Plano Library fundraiser in February, 1993.

The Waldrep family: Mom and Dad, sisters Carole (right) and Terry (left) and Kent on his fortieth birthday at home in Plano.

The Waldrep heirs. Sons Trey (six) and Charley (three) shown here in November, 1993.

Part Three

Hope is not optimism; it is a state of the soul.

✧ CHAPTER TEN ✧

THE BIRTH OF A CHARITY

The Waldreps proceeded slowly through customs. Finally they completed the formalities and a huge pair of metal doors at the end of the hallway inched open. Behind those doors, tier upon tier of media folks waited, the ones in front kneeling. Hundreds of bulbs began flashing, lighting the room like the Leningrad sky whitened by fireworks.

Waves of people let out a clamorous cheer.

Kent triumphantly raised his arms as family and friends swarmed him. Greetings continued until the pandemonium quieted enough for a barrage of inquiries to begin.

With his sisters, his niece, and Terry Stanford behind him, Kent answered them all, sometimes demonstrating the new arm movements. "I'm realistic," he replied to one question, "but one day I *will* walk again."

"Are you bitter about not having this therapy sooner?" a reporter asked.

Kent collected his thoughts before answering, "I don't want to get in a fight with the neurosurgeons, but things have got to be changed in this country. Our doctors have been narrow-minded. The Soviets proved them wrong. We don't have a monopoly on research."

Another reporter called, "What were your Soviet doctors like?"

"They were unbelievable men and women with an incredible, unique capability of combining medical professionalism with compassion. They were straightforward the whole time."

"What would you say to others who want similar treatment?"

"I want to help people — anyone — with my physical therapy program. It's foolish not to try."

Again he paused and then continued, "My condition doesn't just paralyze me. It confines my mom and my dad — my whole family. It's the same for all people confined to a wheelchair.

147

"I know I've said it, but the hopeless attitude perpetuated by the medical community in this country has *got* to be changed. There's a better way. A *much* better way," he added.

They asked more, and he amplified his answers. Finally, his parents moved to end it.

"What's it like to come home so successful?" a last reporter asked.

Kent grinned. "I'm *so* glad to be home," he answered. "Though the Russian people — the medical staff and everyone — were so friendly and supportive, I'm glad to be with my family, glad to be home. Every day is special to me now."

They left the airport and drove immediately to McDonald's, where Kent ate the best quarter-pounder in the world. The meal was rushed, however, as somehow the airline had crushed his wheelchair and it barely held him up through the press conference. Ah, he thought, to sleep in my own bed.

His sister Carole had put together a scrapbook while he was gone. It contained the news articles concerning the Russia trip. The burgeoning book overflowed with stories from all over the world. The coverage was so extensive! No wonder hordes of press covered his arrival both in London and here.

And the public response didn't stop. When they reached home, the phone was ringing. And ringing. And ringing. Now and then the caller was a relative or friend, but most of the calls came from paralyzed people and their families, asking about the treatments. How, when, why, where, and who? the questions ran the journalistic gamut as people from *everywhere* grasped at each bit of information concerning the treatments, searching for even a shred of hope.

Good Morning America asked Kent to fly to New York for an interview two days after his homecoming. I just *can't,* he thought, and declined. Tom Brokaw and *The Today Show* called as well and arranged to broadcast Kent live from KXAS-TV in Fort Worth.

On the morning of the telecast, Kent felt rested from being home and invigorated by all the calls and letters. The questions focused on the Russian approach versus the U.S. approach.

"Basically, the FDA is dragging its feet in approving the enzyme treatments," he said to Brokaw and to the world. "There's no reason the treatments shouldn't be available in the U.S."

That oughta set those neurosurgeons to cackling again, he thought as they drove home. Well, it was past time things got stirred up concerning this issue.

For weeks, the phone rang. All day and into the night. Friends came and helped receive the calls. In order to eat they took the receiver off the hook. It rang at all hours with callers from distant time zones.

"This Grand Central Station stuff is ridiculous," Kent said finally. "There *has* to be a more centralized way to do this."

Denise nodded. "Like put together and send out a mailing covering all the common questions?"

"Yeah. For starters."

His mother stared at him. "What are you thinking?"

"I'm not sure yet. But it'll wait till after the holidays."

Which it did. Christmas was particularly joyous that year. The traditional Yuletide fare rivaled any meal ever served. Funny, he thought, how food seems unimportant until you spend a month eating boiled goulash.

Also in December, an article about his trip appeared in *Time* magazine. And Grand Prairie sponsored a "Kent Waldrep Day."

Local and national press people kept calling or just appearing at the front door. One morning, Kent awakened to the glaring lights of a TV camera at the foot of his bed. Why Denise, with full knowledge of how persnickety he was about "the hair," let those newspeople in was one of life's great mysteries. With gritted teeth, he sailed through the interview.

He went on Larry King's radio show, and *Look* magazine interviewed him. Agents from all over the country contacted him, including some of the biggest in the entertainment industry. Some offered book and movie deals; some promoted speaking tours and motivational tapes. Al and Denise urged caution, but what could any of this hurt?

The medical community might belittle him, but the rest of the world stayed staunchly in Kent's corner.

His mom decided she needed Al around more, so they bought a meat market in Grand Prairie. All went well and they did have more flexibility until the butcher smarted-off and Al fired him. So his dad called a butcher friend for a crash course in the profession. That, coupled with Al's work in the market before the firing, did the trick. Soon his dad cut the most beautiful meat around, and though the hours were long and the work hard, the little shop thrived.

When 1979 began, Kent hit the ground rolling. He and his folks compiled a four-page letter summarizing the Russian treatment, exercise, and hospital information and began mailing it. They still read every letter received, and if someone needed something extra or different, Kent included a note.

"Why *is* there no national charity for this kind of information?" he asked Denise again. "No 'Muscular Dystrophy Association' for spinal cord research in the United States?"

Denise sealed another envelope and said, "You'd think the National Spinal Cord Injury Foundation would be a good resource for this kind of information."

"All they're interested in is perfecting wheel chairs," Kent answered moodily. He'd contacted the organization based in New England with a branch in Fort Worth — before leaving for Leningrad. Jim Grey, the local chapter director, considered himself the local disability guru and kept the group's focus on service delivery. That wasn't Kent's main concern.

So he started digging — calling all the organizations dealing with paralysis and asking questions of anyone involved in nonprofit work. He uncovered one private nonprofit group in Washington, D.C. — the Paralysis Cure Research Foundation. It invested less than $100,000 per year in research. The Paralyzed Veterans of America was another, but it focused most of its research on rehabilitation issues.

No group was creating enough national awareness about paralysis to generate the millions of dollars needed to propel research forward. What was the problem?

Kent found that in 1979 the National Institutes of Health (NIH) allocated less than $7 million to paralysis cure research. But they earmarked *billions* of dollars for cancer research and hundreds of millions to heart disease, diabetes, multiple sclerosis, muscular dystrophy, and every other major disease afflicting humankind. But when it came to a cure for paralysis, they provided no strategy and offered no hope.

On Valentine's Day, Ron Turcotte, the jockey who had ridden Secretariat to the Triple Crown, paid Kent a visit. A spill during a race the previous spring had left Ron paraplegic. He and Kent struck up a phone-friendship after Ron called concerning the Russian treatments.

Ron voiced the same dismay over the lack of organized research. He, too, would gather any information possible and would work with Kent to increase public awareness of spinal cord injuries.

On February 26 Kent traveled to Charlottesville, Virginia, to participate on a panel sponsored by the University of Virginia Law School entitled "Is Medicine in the U.S. Over-regulated?"

For God's sake, Kent thought, looking around at the panel — a group of medical "professionals" and me. Am I fresh bait for this group or what? He looked at his mom in the crowd and grinned. Bring on the lions.

Denise Waldrep sat in the audience, watching as her son prepared to be shredded by a panel of medical experts during this "discussion" sponsored by the legal forum. Ron Turcotte sat beside her. The former jockey looked pale and as nervous as she felt.

On the panel with Kent sat Dr. Karl Kao, a neurosurgeon from Georgetown University. Bill Vodra of the U.S. Food and Drug Administration sat next to him, and Peggy David from University Towers Rehabilitation Center was on the other side. By Kent sat Dr. John Jane, chairman of the Neurosurgery Department at the University of Virginia Medical School. Oh, brother.

The discussion began, and immediately the physicians scoffed at the idea of a cure for paralysis.

Kent responded with, "I went to Russia with a hope. And that hope was realized."

Dr. Jane stared flatly at Kent, his eyebrows and mouth forming parallel vertical lines.

"What we need," Kent continued, "is a coordinated federal government effort to find a cure for paralysis."

The others stated there was no need for that. Some audience members jeered them.

Bill Vodra said the enzyme treatments Kent received had not been proven effective for relief of paralysis victims. Denise bit her tongue. Paralysis *victims*.

Dr. Jane seconded Vodra's claim. "Two separate American research projects seeking to verify the Russians reported that results with en-

151

zyme treatments have been unsuccessful. They have found no validity whatsoever in those experiments. The drug has absolutely no effect."

Ron Turcotte put his hand on Denise's arm to keep her from rising. She bit down harder on her tongue.

Kent, smiling, said, "The enzyme treatments are an aid in the improvement of paralysis, not the total cure. By the time I left, I could feel my left leg and move it when the masseuse stimulated the nerve. It was almost a natural feeling. Now I can tell you where my legs are without looking. If you bend my toes, I can tell you which way. I can feel the floor under my feet when I stand in the walker.

"And you're telling me this isn't progress?" The audience cheered.

"Coincidence," one of the doctors claimed. A booming boo arose from the crowd.

Kent went on to explain the Russian program, receiving full support from the audience. The neurosurgeons were looking awfully bad, Denise thought, loosening her tongue clamp.

"It's not that American doctors don't care," Kent said. "They really *do* feel it's hopeless. They believe they have to take all your hope away to get you ready for the rest of your life in a wheelchair.

"But a wrong is being done," he continued. "The rehab doctors are doing as much to handicap the spinal cord injured as anyone else. The limits the doctors are setting are theirs, not ours."

He paused a moment as the crowd clapped.

Then Kent concluded, "That, combined with the fact of so little funding for spinal cord research, has caused me to plan to establish a center for such research. I went to Russia for hope. It's time I bring some of that hope home."

Tears streamed down Denise's cheeks. How unflappable her boy was. How much he would need his tenacity. These doctors, and those like them around the country, would take an eternity to be swayed. But they were just beginning the battle with Kent Waldrep, and he had just begun to fight. They rose to leave and Denise's tongue felt sore and raw. She had almost bitten through it.

Kent sat at his desk at TCU, unable to believe what his investigations unearthed. The treatments he received in Leningrad were originally

152

researched in the U.S. by Dr. William Windle in the 1950s. After several years, however, the government decided the research wasn't progressing fast enough, and the funding was dropped. Other countries, including the Soviet Union, renewed the studies, persisting to the point where new and promising treatments were now available to spinal cord–injured persons.

No wonder the U.S. medical community wanted none of this: they dropped the ball and sat on their butts while other researchers succeeded in the quest. Professional egos strike again.

He related this to his folks that evening, as he, Denise, and some friends played bridge.

"This can't surprise you, son," Al called from the kitchen where he cooked for the bridge players. The phone rang and Al answered.

"Kent," he said, "it's Jim Grey."

"Evening, Jim," Kent said. "What's happening in Cowtown?"

"Kent my boy," Jim began, "I heard about you causing that stink in Virginia. I got some ideas about how you can work with the NSCIF."

Kent listened as Grey laid out his big plan for raising money. The man was more than clear: the group's power structure would run everything and use the money for rehab technology. When Kent inquired about researching a cure, Grey laughed.

"What did he want?" Denise asked when Kent returned to the table.

He shook his head and answered, "Wants me to be the poster child for paralysis rehab."

"He's getting scared you're gonna take away some of his business," Al said. "Probably heard you were planning to start your own foundation instead of working with his."

"Mom," Kent said, gazing evenly into her eyes, "it's time."

And so they began.

Throughout the spring of 1979, Kent researched and called and contacted dozens of people in nonprofit organizations. The more he delved into the idea of his own foundation, the more flack came his way. Touching some nerves, he reasoned.

Dr. Robert Jackson, president of the National Paraplegia Foundation, attacked Kent in a national interview.

"No one can mend busted cords," Jackson said. "Waldrep's trip to

153

the Soviet Union did a grave disservice to other spinal cord injury patients by instilling false hope."

Ha! There's the old false hope argument again. It had become a catch-phrase for anything Kent did outside the status quo. He smiled. The rebuttal meant he was hitting home.

Kent worked tirelessly. He had lots of time. He'd quit seeing Marti, and Terry again drifted away. She called from time to time, but she'd moved to Houston and was dating yet another guy whom she professed to "really like," though it seemed this guy treated her badly. She phoned when things were rough — which was often — relating some pretty awful stuff. But she stayed in the relationship.

Her whole life lay ahead, she told Kent. She had all these dreams — dreams of marriage and children, of a career. How excited she'd been when he walked in Russia! But then he returned and the same problems existed between them.

Kent happened to hear a country song that must've been written just for him. He immediately bought the tape, listening to the song over and over, until the lyrics were stamped on his brain:

> I can still feel your fingers touching my face,
> your breath on my cheek, your soft embrace —
> feelings eternity cannot erase.
> But don't look for the signs
> cause you'll find not a trace.
> Because I'm stronger now than I've ever been before.
> I'm breaking through walls, and knocking down doors.
> Nothing's gonna stop me from what I'm looking for.
> If I have to search this world from shore to shore.
> I can't say there's not been times I've hurt,
> But I can say there's times I've been through worse,
> And, yes, you'll always have a place in my heart . . .
> I'll just put it with the other broken parts.
> Because I'm stronger now than I've ever been before.
> I'm breaking through walls, and knocking down doors.
> Nothing's gonna stop me from what I'm looking for.
> If I have to search this world from shore to shore.

He still missed Terry, but a little less each day. And he *was* stronger than he'd ever been before. Now, with God's help, he planned to knock down lots of doors.

And Terry would marry this guy. He who would never treat her as she deserved to be treated, would run around on her and break her heart. But there wasn't a thing Kent could do about it. Summer approached, and he vowed to let Terry Stanford go.

So he put all his energies into the foundation, and on June 15, 1979, the Kent Waldrep International Spinal Cord Research Foundation (KWISCRF, what a mouthful, Kent thought) was born. Where other foundations focused on rehabilitation, his planned to channel funds into researchers and laboratories worldwide. They would actively lobby for increased government funding to strengthen the commitment and support from the corporate and public sectors of American society — all in order to research a cure for paralysis.

Of course, he had little clue as to what he was doing. But he did know enough to ask. He finally signed with the biggest literary agency in the country, and they sent writers down. As of yet, no words on paper materialized, but these things took time.

The day before Kent announced the formation of his foundation, both he and Bob Hurt (a race car driver who had been paralyzed and also trekked to Russia for treatments) were examined by a pair of doctors from the Paralyzed Veterans Association and the V.A.

After performing one test — drawing needles across Kent and Bob — the doctors proclaimed no improvement on either. They didn't even do some of the more routine things I've received in other exams, Kent thought. Not to mention that these doctors hadn't examined either of them *before* their trips to Russia. What a joke.

The literary agency put him in touch with a Hollywood P.R. firm, which designed an impressive press kit, brochures, and supporting materials for the KWISCRF. Kent traveled to Hollywood, enlisting the support of famous actors who pledged to carry the foundation's banner. Meeting Jim Garner, Clint Eastwood, Lauren Bacall, and a host of others sent him into the unreality zone. Though Denise and Al attempted to keep his feet on the ground, Kent liked flying close to the sun.

Besides, on one trip he played a part in *Days of Our Lives,* doing

155

a bedroom scene with Deidra Hall. He couldn't understand, however, why his mom and dad weren't as excited about the hoopla as he was. Soon though, the book would be written and published, followed by a movie and then everyone would see that these show-biz people weren't nearly the piranhas they were reported to be.

Kent produced a plan of action for the foundation, devised a three-year budget describing how the money would be spent, and included a list of prospective scientists to help guide the research program.

Relying on his Hollywood contacts, he planned to produce a black-tie fund-raiser just three months after opening the foundation's doors. Though he knew diddly-squat about fund-raising, there was no time like the present to learn.

He ran into brick walls trying to launch the event in such a short time. Each detail produced struggle. The big promoters promised lots of support, but never actually did much. When the Hollywood types visited, Al left the house. And to date, writing for the book had yet to begin.

Okay, Kent decided, there's more than one way to pop a cork. Let's revamp some.

So they postponed the gala until November and planned like crazy.

Meanwhile, Jim Grey and his group started making noise. Grey hadn't been so happy about Kent forming his own foundation, but then neither had any of the others. We don't want to split the dollars, they all maintained. But their dollars were going to rehab. He earmarked his for researching a cure.

"Yeah, we're going at a break-neck pace," Kent said to one reporter as the date for the event approached. "My mom and a group of really dedicated volunteers are working like possessed people."

"Why Fort Worth?" the reporter asked, "rather than Dallas or Los Angeles or some other city known for hosting big galas?"

"Fort Worth is the logical site for this," Kent answered. "It's home to tens of thousands of TCU alumni, friends, and fans. We're looking for about a thousand people."

A thousand guests, he thought, hanging up the phone. At a $100 a plate, that should put a few research dollars in the bank! That night, Kent dreamed of playing golf — and of running.

Finally the fund-raiser came together. Denise, ever the Trojan, and the other volunteers had everything in line. One of those, Jane Burgland, was especially helpful. She also kept trying to introduce Kent to her daughter, Lynn, though they kept missing one another.

The Monday before the fund-raiser on Thursday, a reporter from the *Fort Worth Star-Telegram,* Barbara Johnson, interviewed Kent. The press had given him lots of coverage, publicizing both the foundation and the event. Good deal, Kent reasoned, this will just add more fuel to our growing fire.

She asked him the usual questions about the gala, and they chatted amiably.

The day before the event, her story broke. Huge, front-page headlines on the *Star-Telegram* proclaimed:

WALDREP FOUNDATION QUESTIONED

"The foundation founded by Kent Waldrep to raise money for spinal cord injury research is not the nonprofit, tax-exempt organization it claims to be," the story began. "Furthermore, a number of the prominent scientists listed as membership-elect to the foundation's advisory committee did not know about the foundation or the committee. Some of them angrily objected to the foundation's use of their names, saying they oppose Waldrep's efforts." One researcher, who asked not to be identified, said he'd seen "a dozen or more small foundations like Waldrep's come and go over the years."

Kent grew red. His heartbeat quickened and his muscles clenched and he wanted to scream.

The story continued, saying that the foundation was not registered as a nonprofit corporation with the secretary of state in Austin, nor did it have tax-exempt status. It also quoted Jim Grey issuing a disclaimer concerning Waldrep's group because he received calls indicating that the public was confusing the two groups. Grey said he believed Waldrep's group was "misrepresenting" itself. And the story reported Kent's salary as $32,400 per year.

Kent did scream. Who would *do* this to them? *Why* would anyone do it? None of it was true. They *did* have their nonprofit registration with the state. And they *had* applied for their tax-exempt status with the IRS — all the paperwork was in order and now only the formality of the IRS exempting them was left. And him making $32,400 a year?

When he actually drew $500 a month? Math was hard, but for the life of him, Kent couldn't make those two figures balance.

And that woman never questioned him about any of this during the interview. She already had her slam story written and spoke with him just as a formality. The only thing true in the whole article was that they didn't have a solicitation permit from the city, and hell, he never even knew of that requirement. Dammit.

Kent read it again. The professionals angry about being named to the *prospective* scientific advisory board had one thing in common — they all sat on the NSCIF Board. Hmm. Jim Grey loudly vocalized his opposition to Kent's foundation. Jim Grey had once written for the *Star-Telegram* and still claimed lots of friends there. Well, Kent had friends too, and he'd get to the bottom of this. But first, he must save the gala.

He called a press conference and refuted the claims, showing proof of the misinformation. It might be too late to undo the damage, but he could save the event.

Which he did. The city's dignitaries rallied around him. Fort Worth's mayor, Woodie Woods, came, as did many of the community's leaders. The sports journalists, including Verne Lundquist and Randy Galloway, attended. So did a host of the Hollywood actors involved — even after the person committed to underwriting their airfare pulled out at the last minute. Though the slam story knocked the fund-raiser to its knees, they still pulled it off and put much needed money into the bank. Only Channel 5, the NBC affiliate in Fort Worth covered the event. The other television stations ignored it.

The day after the gala, the *Star-Telegram* printed a retraction (which did *not* appear on page one). Kent sat at his desk, the sickness in his belly growing. Part of him wanted to sue the paper for the complete falsehoods and conspiracy behind the story. But again, so many folks rallied behind him, producing new stories portraying the truth, what was the point? The event was over; no lawsuit could undo what was done. And he learned so much through this process. The next one would be bigger and better.

The strife sparked a lot of press. *4 Country Reporter* at the CBS affiliate in Dallas came to do a story on the whole Kent Waldrep controversy. After his last experience, he agreed to it only because the assistant producer was Jane Burgland's daughter — the very one Kent kept missing these past months.

Actually, he had briefly met Lynn Burgland at the fund-raiser, but with so many people and so much pandemonium, he remembered little about her except that she was cute and had short, bouncy-blond hair.

They traveled around in his van, and she allowed that this was her first on-camera work. Fine. Her laughter was infectious, and it lit up her clear blue-green eyes. Though this might be her first TV rattle out of the box, her self-confidence put him completely at ease. She asked all the right questions. By the time the interview ended, he couldn't keep his gaze from her.

Kent wheeled with her into the driveway and out to her van. "Your mom's been trying to introduce us for a long time," Kent said.

Lynn laughed. "My mother has just loved you forever. You've really got her fooled."

"I'm an ace with older women."

She laughed again and he rubbed his chin. Was it too soon to ask her out? So much time passed since he'd done that. She seemed to like him but other girls had liked him too. . . .

Lynn leaned against the van, cocking her strong jaw sideways and smiled. "I bet you're an ace with *all* women," she said and paused. "Besides, Mom says you're the most eligible bachelor around."

Inwardly he groaned but replied, "Yeah, right. I'm the John Travolta of Grand Prairie. Dance with me if you can."

Lynn laughed, eyes sparkling. "Well," she said finally, opening her door, "I guess I best be going." She hesitated a minute, looking around the yard and then back to Kent.

Everything inside him locked and no words emerged. She stepped into the van.

"I, um, would like to see the tape when you get finished," he said, wanting to kick himself.

She nodded. "I'll bring you one."

They said goodbye. As Kent watched her drive away, a funny sensation waltzed through his body. No, he thought, don't even think about it. But he stared where her van had vanished down the street and forgot to think of Terry Stanford.

159

✧ CHAPTER ELEVEN ✧

A CURE IS POSSIBLE

A week later, Kent dialed Lynn's number. "Hi there," he said to her cheerful hello. "How's life in TV land?"

"Video crazy," she replied. "But your tape's about done."

"When can I see it?"

"Hm," she said and paused. "I'll bring a copy by day after tomorrow. How's that?"

"Great. I can't wait to see, umm, the show. How'd it turn out?"

Lynn laughed. "Real well, I think. You can judge for yourself."

Then he blurted, "You want to go to a movie sometime?"

"Sure," she answered, and Kent felt the warmth of her smile over the phone. "That'd be fun."

They said goodbye, and Kent sat still for a few minutes, feeling as if he were fifteen years old and had just asked out the senior prom queen. Which of course, he had, way back when. And she said yes, too. For one glorious time after his freshman high school year, Kent dated an "older woman" before the family moved to dreaded Alvin. What confidence he possessed as a teenager. But a wall of white water had rushed under him since then.

Two days later Kent fidgeted as he waited for Lynn and the tape. He and Brad, Terry Lynn's husband, were rummaging through foundation correspondence when Lynn breezed in, video in hand.

Dressed in blue velvet, she looked like an angel. Her short, blond hair shone in the office light. Again, he acted like a schoolboy until she left.

"I'm gonna marry her," he said to Brad after Lynn walked out. Brad stared as if Kent had just gulped down a fourth hurricane at Pat O'Brien's in New Orleans.

Another week passed before he mustered the confidence to call her back, and this time *she* invited *him* out. TCU was sponsoring a fund-

160

raising event, the Frog Bowl, which enlisted area journalists to bowl for charity. Yes, the perfect date — they both would know people and feel at ease.

Unfortunately, upon arrival they found the bowling alley positioned on the second floor of a building with no elevator. So Kent left for a friend's house, returning later to pick up Lynn. They ate supper at Cheddar's and talked for four hours. As he dropped her back home, Kent lightly kissed her lips and then drove into the darkness feeling giddy and free. That night he dreamt of winning the hundred-yard dash.

Throughout the next weeks, Lynn and Kent went out often. How comfortable he was with her; how cheering her laughter.

Storm clouds churned on the horizon, though: the foundation was floundering. The *Star-Telegram* accusations (which the paper retracted in full by January) killed his fund-raising efforts. Retractions never make big headlines, and the initial slam-story stayed stuck in people's minds. The KWISCRF was in deep trouble.

So in January of 1980, Kent closed his offices and moved the foundation into the house to lower overhead. He did raise some money, and started an ongoing dialogue with research scientists.

The foundation *had* put capital into research already, albeit nothing like what Kent hoped for. More and more scientists started lending support, supplying much needed credibility as well.

Plus, Kent had made friends with some of the Dallas Cowboys players during their summer training camp in Thousand Oaks, California. He loved the feel of football camp, the aromas of liniment and sweat flooding his senses with memories. Several of the players sought him out, wanting to collaborate with the foundation. Cliff Harris kept in touch. He offered to work with Kent on the next fund-raiser and pledged to make contacts after post-season play was completed.

Kent knew he was on the correct course, could feel the foundation moving in the right directions, and knew it would prosper in the long run. The short run was what worried him.

He also started speaking to schools and churches. Often Lynn traveled along. Though her television schedule remained hectic, she always carved out time for him.

Talking to the kids invigorated Kent. They were so honest. Staring openly, children asked what they really wanted to know concerning disability — much of which centered around going to the bathroom — unlike the grown-ups who hid behind masks when they spoke with him. Often adults avoided his gaze.

New shoots of emerald green grasses sprouted through the country-side. Buds grew into leaves on the trees and flowers bloomed, their heady-sweet scents filling the air. As the world blossomed into spring-time, Kent fell deeply in love with Lynn.

This happened so quickly, he thought. They grew close so fast. Was it too hasty? Was he setting himself up once more for heartache? Could Lynn cope with him as he was, when neither Terry nor Katie could? And how to talk with Lynn about all this, *how in the world?*

One weekend, Terry came to town and took him to lunch as she often did. They talked and laughed and joked before the conversation became more serious.

"I'll always love you, Kent," Terry said. "You're the flame that will never die. But what we had was fantasy — we had each other when we were young and beautiful."

Kent cocked his head and replied, "I don't know about you, but *I'm* still beautiful."

Terry stared hard at him and did not laugh. "But you equate me with those times when you were whole," she said, slugging the table with her fist. "You equate me with feelings of walking and excitement and fun. All those emotions got mixed up in you. You can't tell where I begin and walking ends."

Listening silently, he saw the sadness in her eyes. She's a little off right here, he thought. *I'm* not the one who's confused. But there's no way to explain that either. Terry's mind's made up — muddled or not.

"Still," she continued, more softly now, "we have the purest form of love — a pure emotional and spiritual love, not a physical one. And we'll always have each other for that."

Kent felt no sadness as they parted that day, only warmth and love for one of his best friends. And Terry was right about a thing or two — the bond between them would never be broken. One point, however, she missed by a mile: he felt whole now. And the reason for that was Lynn.

In May of 1980, Kent again took Lynn to Cheddar's — the site of

162

their first date. They'd talked informally about the future — and of marriage. When he proposed, ring and all, Lynn was not surprised. She said yes. Her heart was already set on a Christmas wedding.

"I only wonder if," Kent began the next day as he and Lynn sat on the Waldreps' back porch, "if . . . hell, I don't know how to put this."

"Just say it Kent," Lynn said. Her blue eyes, highlighted with green flecks, glistened in the sun's bright radiance. So clear and open, they invited him to confide.

He breathed deeply and started again, "If you can really cope . . . with me, and the reality of my situation. I mean, Terry couldn't, and she loved me too."

"Well," Lynn said without hesitation, "I can't tell you for a *fact* that I can, because I don't know exactly what all's involved. But Kent, I never knew you *out* of your wheelchair, like Terry did. That's the main difference — she knew you as you *were*, not as you are now."

Kent rubbed his eyes with the back of his hand.

"Let's do it this way," Lynn continued, "why don't I move in here with y'all and learn how to take care of you?"

Kent raised his eyebrows. Lynn's even gaze did not falter.

So in she moved. Immediately, Denise involved Lynn in all aspects of Kent's care. His future wife took everything in stride, more so in fact than he did. Some things were awfully personal. The most embarrassing was Lynn attending to bathroom duties. There was, after all, a reason bathrooms had doors to close — but he could live with that. To his amazement, Lynn could live with it all, too. Not ever did she say — nor as far as he could discern even think — "When you walk again."

Lynn tackled the responsibility and the relationship. Kent found himself divulging his deepest fears — something he never before could do. Though his family hadn't considered the idea of his ever living a normal life — or more specifically, marrying — they soon accepted both the notion and Lynn. Her devotion to him was absolute.

Now if they could just pull off a Christmas wedding when every church and reception hall had been reserved for months, Kent would be a husband. He was marrying a remarkable woman who truly loved him for himself, of that he had no doubt. Could life get any better?

✧

163

Lynn drove down the interstate toward Grand Prairie. She'd just quit her job with *4 Country Reporter,* to work full-time with the foundation. The timing was right. She considered quitting before — to return to school and proceed with a master's degree in speech pathology. After learning sign language and working with the hearing-impaired, she needed more than journalism to maintain her interest.

Helping with the foundation was perfect. Terry Lynn's husband, Brad, quit right after the *Star-Telegram* debacle, and Kent let his secretary go when the funds ran low. Now he really needed Lynn — to travel with and care for him. He needed her in a way in which she had never felt. And that warmed her soul.

Plus, she wanted to spend every second with him. Before Kent, she hadn't seriously dated anyone for a long while. After they met, no other man interested her. It was meant to be. Lynn never analyzed nor feared the decision to marry. She loved him, plain and simple. And rather than being a drain, his need enriched her life.

4 Country Reporter brought them together, and she felt grateful for that. Of course, Kent thought her involvement in his story segment to be purely coincidence. He needn't know she instigated the whole thing after connecting with him at the ill-fated fund-raiser.

"It's great to finally meet you," he had said that night. Though strong and handsome, a sweetness shone from his eyes. "Your mom has been saying so many wonderful things about you, I figured you for a princess. I can see I was right."

That was about the extent of their interaction at the event as *everyone* wanted a minute with Kent. Soon after, however, Lynn presented a sketch of the piece to her producer. It worked out pretty well, all in all.

She pulled in front of the house and cut her motor at the same time Denise did.

"Hi, sweetie," Denise said, hugging her as they walked inside. "Here, let me carry something for you." Denise grabbed the satchel with Lynn's desk contents.

Kent spoke on the phone as the women walked in. He frowned, his voice raised, and Lynn looked at Denise, who shook her head and laughed. Kent could be tough to work for. His total dedication caused him constantly to brainstorm new projects — additional folks to contact, more research to explore. Kent toiled harder and longer for the foundation than Lynn had ever seen anyone work on anything. She wasn't just marrying a man, but an entire cause.

Two months later, after a long day answering foundation correspondence, Lynn sat with Denise in the kitchen drinking iced tea. The hot July days kept everyone inside, and the cool drink provided sorely needed refreshment.

"I spoke with your mother today," Denise said.

"You two've become great friends, huh?" Lynn replied as Denise refilled both tea glasses. "Thanks."

"She's such a go-getter," Denise said. "She's already involved Kent in the Reagan fund-raiser. Now she wants him working for the administration."

Lynn laughed and said, "That's Mom." She rubbed her forehead with one palm.

"I told her that you already had Kent's routine down pat. She wasn't a bit surprised."

"You've been a good teacher."

Denise folded her hands on the table. She cocked her head slightly and said, "I know it hasn't been easy. You just can't know what this is like until, well, until you do it. And this had to be a huge adjustment for you — living alone all these years and being so independent. But Jane said you're used to being with the family every weekend anyway."

"There was *always* lots of activity around our house," Lynn answered, laughing again. "But you and Al have made this so easy. And shoot, with everybody working all week, it's not that much different than going to my folks' on the weekend."

"Taking care of Kent's different, though."

Lynn looked her soon-to-be-mother-in-law square in the eyes. "None of it's hard," she said, "except the extra hours it takes in the morning to get him ready. How have you done it and gotten yourself ready and gotten to work on time to boot?"

Denise shrugged. "I guess I'm so used to it, I've forgotten how it was before."

Lynn nodded. Yes, this would take some getting used to, but one day she'd feel the same. "The only thing that really bugs me," she began, "is that each little hair has to be perfectly in place."

"And he looks at it from every angle," Denise agreed.

"I just love it when you've worked on it and worked on it, and then he takes the mirror and says, 'What's this one hair doing sticking out over here?'" Lynn said pulling a short strand of her own hair to the side.

"That doesn't get any better."

"Do you sometimes want to strangle him?"

Laughing, Denise patted Lynn's arm and said, "Mothers are more patient."

"Or when you've gotten him all dressed and he points and says, 'My belt's not *exactly* lined up with my shirt buttons; move it one centimeter to the left.'"

Denise nodded. "That's Kent."

"Has he always been so persnickety about his appearance?"

"Only since he could talk. Especially that hair."

"I think I'll get him a burr."

"He'd shoot you dead," Denise said matter-of-factly. "His haircut worried him more right after the accident than his broken neck did."

"I think it still does."

They joked about Kent for a while longer, before Denise asked, "Are you two going to Terry's wedding?"

"Um hm," Lynn answered. "And I think we're gonna get with her before the wedding, too. Kent wants us all to spend time together."

"That'd be wonderful," Denise said. "She's played such a big part in his life."

"I know. He's worried about the guy she's marrying, too. Says he'll hurt her in the end."

Denise frowned. "It's hard *not* to worry about her." Then she stood abruptly and offered more tea. "Oh," she said, "we're playing bridge tonight, you in?"

Smiling, Lynn nodded. That was one of the advantages to living here — always enough people around for a bridge game. She loved the resonance of a full house. And, she thought with an inward chuckle, it made up for Kent's hair proclivities.

They did go to Terry Stanford's wedding that August. Sitting in the back row, Kent felt very weird. He worried about Terry; there was

166

something dark about her groom's personality. When she walked down the aisle, her gaze fell upon Kent. Her eyes were opaque and troubled.

Had things worked out differently, it mighta been me up there, he thought. All her worries about him walking tap-danced through his mind. He glanced sideways at Lynn. She still looked like an angel, the muted church lights forming a halo around her blond head. God, he loved this woman here beside him. But would she start to brood about him walking as well? She hadn't so far, even saying that she'd have a problem at this point if he *did* suddenly walk, as she would no longer know him.

They didn't hang around after the "I do's," didn't go to the reception. When Kent closed his eyes that night, he thanked God life unfolded this way, thanked God for sending him Lynn.

Their own wedding plans moved along. Now if only the foundation could get back on its feet.

Lots of folks lent support — from movie stars to scientists, football heroes such as recently retired Dallas Cowboys Roger Staubach and Cliff Harris, to families who dealt with disabilities every day. Cliff had taken to traveling with Kent, giving speeches to churches and civic organizations. The companionship was wonderful, and Captain Crash, as Cliff was known in his safety-playing days, drew lots of response.

Cliff had retired that year after his third bout with temporary paralysis on the field. He'd been impressed by Kent's discussions of what strides the Russians were making and how much more could be done with American technology, if the AMA would only listen.

In a speech one day to a group of Midland businessmen, Kent listened as Cliff told them, with fire in his eyes and conviction in his voice, just that.

"I am an athlete," Cliff said, "and Kent's an athlete. I got involved in his organization first, to help him as one athlete to another. There's a camaraderie between us on that level.

"But now I know what it's like for Kent to get up in the mornings and brush his teeth. And I know it doesn't have to be this way.

"Kent Waldrep has a vision — a vision for victory. He has seen a little ray of hope, and is showing that hope to the world. Kent knows, and now I know and we want you to understand as well, that with just this tiny bit of hope, we *can* accomplish the impossible.

"Kent has been told, 'you can't do it' — which just makes him that much more determined. From the results of his trip to Russia, Kent knows that it is possible for him and millions like him to walk again. Kent Waldrep magnifies the idea that dreams can come true — that together, we can make possible the impossible, that we *can* do it. He personifies the American way."

As the crowd cheered Kent thought, God bless you, Cliff Harris. Cliff was no longer working for a charity, but rather with a vision for victory. Cliff understood.

But even with this sort of help, after the blow delivered during the fund-raiser the previous year the foundation went deeply into debt. Kent borrowed money to keep it afloat. All the good intentions in the world, however, wouldn't pay off the bank note. But they had come too far to look back, so he racked his brain for avenues to pursue. He prayed a lot, too.

And he played a little politics thanks to Lynn's mother, Jane. One of Jane's friends, Pat Jacobsen, was a key Republican fund-raiser, working with Michael Deaver through the Reagan campaign. Kent met many of Reagan's staffers. Pat asked if Kent might be interested in working with the Reagan administration's policies on the handicapped (assuming they won). What a hoot, Kent thought.

As the fall progressed, the foundation hung on by its fingernails. There must be a way. There just must.

A smaller but no less significant setback occurred that year as well. A joint conference between the American and Soviet spinal cord researchers was to be held in Los Angeles, but when the U.S.S.R. invaded Afghanistan, the Soviets cancelled their trip. The conference went the way of the 1980 Olympics, for the Americans anyway. And it was the spinal cord–injured, like the U.S. Olympic athletes, who lost out.

While his foundation dreams struggled, however, his personal life soared. Lynn stood with him through the adversity. Soon they would be married, maybe one day have a child.

The wedding drew nearer. Somehow, Lynn put together all the pieces. Well, almost all. It wouldn't exactly be a Christmas wedding, but December 6 was close enough. She had to find an alternate place for the reception at the last minute, but did so. Kent marveled at her resourcefulness, which made Denise laugh and say, "To live with you, Kent, she's gonna need it." His very own mother said that.

On Lynn's instruction, the florist fashioned her bouquet into a miniature Christmas wreath. All would be more than perfect.

Finally, the day arrived. At the chapel on the Southern Methodist University campus, Kent sat in a side room with his groomsmen — Al, Brad, Lindy Berry, Jim Garner, and Steve Blanchard, an old high-school buddy. They teased about cold feet but he felt none of that. He, like Lynn, was merely delighted the time ultimately arrived and all preparations were done. Lynn's cousin, the Reverend Robert Hasley, would marry them.

The ceremony began. Sitting surrounded by his groomsmen, Kent awaited the wedding march. He had promised not to make Lynn laugh. He repeated the pledge a hundred times to himself — she'd kill him if he hedged. He was not, however, at all certain he could keep the pact.

The music began and bridesmaids floated down the aisle. And last came his bride.

He couldn't see her though. Her body stood hidden behind a Christmas wreath bouquet huge enough to hang on a church steeple. Unseen arms bolstered this creation as styrofoam backing snagged on the pews to each side.

The florist had been confused. Kent mustered enormous will to keep his composure. Lynn gazed anywhere but at him, thank the Lord, or the whole affair would have gone down in shrieks.

The ceremony proceeded unhampered from there. How wonderfully beautiful she is, Kent thought during the vows. What an incredible decision it was to marry her. In the past I've made mistakes, but this is the right thing.

God smiled on them that warm and sunny December day. Everything sparkled. Kent barely remembered the reception; it all played out in a blur of photographs. Terry attended the ceremony, blending vaguely into the background, and then vanished without a word.

Of course, the guys trashed his van — so much so that with all the bird seed and shaving cream *inside,* he and Lynn could hardly get in it. But they did, and after a night spent at the Anatole Hotel, they were off to Hawaii for the honeymoon.

They received many wonderful wedding gifts, but a very special one came from Marvin Gearhart, a KWISCRF board member and dear friend. Marvin gave to the foundation enough stock in Gearhart Industries to pay off the borrowed bank note — enough to keep the foundation alive.

As Kent and Lynn started their life as man and wife, a huge burden lifted. Yes, God in His heaven was surely smiling upon them.

With the foundation back on sound financial footing, Kent and Lynn revved up communications with the scientific community, keeping them abreast of what the foundation was doing and planning to do.

Good news came from a rejuvenated scientific community as well. In the 1950s, William Windle almost single-handedly carried the message that the nervous system could be repaired. After that, however, research funds dried up, due largely to the fact that study of the mammalian spinal cord progressed at a snail's pace.

Then, in 1969, Geoffrey Raisman at the National Institute for Medical Research in London proved new synapses form in the brain after injury. American scientists took note.

In 1970 Windle chaired a meeting sponsored by the National Paraplegia Foundation, where a consensus of prominent neurosurgeons agreed for the first time that based on their research, spinal cord injury need not be permanent. Their message, however, somehow got lost in the mainstream of medical thought. But some researchers heard the segment's report, "It is not a lag in science but in attitude."

No lie, Kent thought, delving deeper into research. He read and read. He found to his chagrin that research into spinal cord injury and repair was painstakingly slow, and not much funding was available.

Still, scientists persisted. In 1977 Dr. Carl Kao, a physician and researcher at George Washington University, experimented with implants of peripheral nerves (sciatic nerves) into the lesioned area of spinal cords in dogs.

Some of Kao's dogs, once paralyzed, were walking. Kent found that peripheral nerve tissue has an intrinsic ability to regenerate, whereas central nervous tissue does not. But the peripheral transplant tissue provides a special chemical environment for the central nervous system's axon growth. Axons, long extensions of nerve fiber, carry action potential from the nerve cell to a target and also carry materials from the nerve terminals back to the nerve cell.

When an axon is cut, proteins required for its regeneration are made available by the nerve cell body. A growth cone forms at the tip of the axon. The axon is prepared to grow and has available a supply of material to do so. It is the environment that surrounds the axon, and not the genetic programming of the axon itself, that prevents regeneration in the mammalian central nervous system.

How long it has taken research to get to this point, Kent thought, the fault being not with the scientists, but because of a basic lack of funds. At the turn of the century, the Spanish scientist Santiago Ramón y Cajal noted that the central nervous cells of dogs and cats, when injured, began to regenerate. After a few days, however, the process stopped.

Now we know he was right, Kent thought. The adult central nervous system has the potential for regeneration but cannot grow again and restore function without intervention or environmental manipulation of some sort.

If the correct environment could be researched, the possibility of spinal cord regeneration in humans was more than a possibility. Funds were needed. Desperately.

In 1979 Wise Young, a researcher from New York University, studied how the environment of the spinal cord plays a part in the mechanisms of recovery.

"It became very clear," Young said, "that the premise of regeneration being a moon shot held by neurosurgeons and clinicians was simply wrong."

Through a federally funded grant, Young began the National Acute Spinal Cord Injury Study. This multicenter experiment sought to compare the effects of methylprednisolone on a large group of patients. Everyone concerned with paralysis, as well as the scientific research community, anxiously awaited Young's findings. Still, the going was so slow.

Unlike other types of studies where ten experiments could be completed in a week, research into paralysis required years and years with one subject. Neither the general public — which provided much of the funding — nor the federal government had much patience with such creeping progress.

Well, he'd keep folks focused on paralysis study. Too much evidence now existed that a cure was truly possible. The requirements were simply twofold: time and money.

About this time, Cliff Harris introduced Kent to Max Williams, a Texas oil man for whom Cliff now worked. Williams contributed much money to the foundation and introduced Kent to someone who made enough of a difference to the KWISCRF that its entire course would be changed.

Pat Holloway was an oil man with a vested interest in paralysis cure research: his daughter had sustained a spinal cord injury. Holloway and his first wife, Linda Allison, jumped into the foundation work with both feet. They contributed *lots* of money, and suddenly the KWISCRF started funding lots of research. The foundation was finally off and running.

Kent had learned some vital lessons. Through Holloway, he learned that the disappointment over the lack of response from the many can be overwhelmed by the generosity and sincerity of one.

And he was coming to know that in its simplest form fund-raising is always leverage. Little dollars can be raised by having a "good" cause and appealing to the hearts of the public. But conquering an issue like paralysis requires big money, which requires big leverage.

More importantly, Kent knew he needed to learn more about fund-raising. There must be folks who could teach him. But where?

One day, the National Society of Fund-Raising Executives contacted him to invite his membership. Never having heard of them, Kent did some checking and found them to be a solid, well-respected organization. Immediately he joined and started attending their seminars. The people couldn't have been nicer nor more helpful. In no time, Kent started truly learning the fund-raising trade.

Doors kept opening. One contact led to another. Influential people introduced him to more influential folks, and respect for his foundation grew. More money poured in, and more research grants were awarded.

Some of the sponsors pointed out that perhaps the revenues for spinal cord research should be combined, that they needed one central organization raising research dollars, not three.

This makes sense, Kent thought. So, with the added leverage that began with the Holloways, Kent contacted the Paralysis Cure Research Foundation and the National Spinal Cord Injury Foundation in mid-1981.

Yes, they were interested. Kent was still big news. People in both organizations agreed that to combine resources under one umbrella would logarithmically strengthen their cause. Negotiations began.

In the fall of 1981, President Reagan nominated Kent to the National Council on the Handicapped. That name's gotta go, Kent thought. The word "handicapped" was not acceptable, but he'd wait for his official appointment to start making noise. "Learning patience in my old age," he said to Lynn, who rolled her eyes. Neither his mother nor his wife attributed that virtue to him.

They completed the paperwork for his appointment, and he was investigated by the IRS and FBI. Once the inquest was completed, the U.S. Senate still had to confirm him.

The first week in November, *People* magazine printed a flattering piece on Kent. Just one week later, his second fund-raiser, the Texas Tycoon Gala, chaired by Clint Murchison, Jr., and his wife, Anne, netted over $100,000. Murchison, the founder and owner of the Dallas Cowboys, combined with Amon Carter, Jr., publisher and owner of the *Fort Worth Star-Telegram* and from one of the founding families of Fort Worth as well, to put the KWISCRF truly on the map.

As 1981 came to a close, Kent knew the merger with the Paralysis Cure Foundation would occur. Participation by the NSCIF, however, looked to be more doubtful. Though the oldest group of its kind, with chapter networks around the country, the organization itself was deeply in debt — to the tune of $200,000, they reported. After an audit, however, the figure was found to be more like a half a million — too big a liability to absorb.

Just before Kent left for Boston for one final negotiation with the NSCIF, he received a call from Milton Petrie's office, saying Mr. Petrie had seen the *People* magazine article, would like to meet Kent, and when could he be there.

"Who is Milton Petrie?" Lynn asked, wrinkling her nose. "I haven't the foggiest," Kent admitted, shaking his head and laughing. "But we're going through New York anyway, so I may as well see him. God knows, benefactors have come from the strangest places."

In New York, Petrie sent a limousine to pick up Kent, Denise, and Lynn. Kent still knew little about the man, except that he owned a big clothing factory. But the Waldreps soon found out more.

Petrie's was a women's clothier, big in the northeast. He had recently started a chain of toy stores as well. It was called Toys 'R' Us.

In the cramped office sat a seventy-something-year-old man, surrounded by papers, gadgets, and hundreds of toys. Kent had never seen such clutter.

"I read your story and want to help you out," Petrie said, cutting right to the chase.

He handed Kent a check for $25,000. He took them to lunch with the head of ABC. The network planned to produce a film about spinal cord injury. And Petrie introduced Kent to Howard Rusk, the godfather of rehabilitation in the U.S.

If this won't add credibility to our new organization, nothing will, Kent thought, traveling home.

What a difference a year makes. Good grief, how far they traveled, the strides they made. And God really did provide benefactors from the oddest places — just when he needed them most. Kent had long since stopped looking gift horses in the mouth, but even he took pause.

The blessings of the past year were immeasurable. And now, with the virtual certainty of forming a new, stronger foundation imminent, Kent took a long, deep breath. 1981 had certainly been a banner year. But merely the beginning. They navigated through some really rough waters, and now the entire ocean spread wide before them.

He couldn't help remembering the Spanish scientist Cajal's words, "Ideas are only fertile to those who feel them passionately and who entrust them all their faith and all their love."

With the abundance of new research unlocking important doors and the foundation growing by leaps and bounds, a cure for paralysis in Kent's lifetime seemed just over the horizon. The course ahead shone clearly and bright.

✧ CHAPTER TWELVE ✧

SCALING A MOUNTAIN AND TUMBLING DOWN

From January until April, Kent and those involved in the Paralysis Cure Research Foundation fine-tuned their merger into the American Paralysis Association. Personalities clashed from the get-go, but Kent always felt that the greater goal of a cure was the most important thing. Egos could be worked out.

Neither Denise nor Lynn shared his optimism, both expressing doubts about the many egos involved. In the end, however, the merger seemed best for their ultimate goal — researching a cure for paralysis. Talks continued with the National Spinal Cord Injury Foundation, but by spring everyone agreed to exclude that organization from the new one.

Finally in April of 1982, the American Paralysis Association held its first meeting in Washington, D.C. Though the national headquarters remained in Kent's Dallas offices, a Washington office would expedite lobbying for federal funds.

Many of his KWISCRF board members joined the new board, including Bear Bryant, George Wallace, Lamar Hunt, Clint Murchison, Cliff Harris, Clint Eastwood, Muhammad Ali, and Roy Campanella. Many of the new members (inherited from the other organization) included people with spinal cord injured children.

From the start, they decided to reorganize the board's structure.

"It'll work better this way, boy," retired Rear Admiral Dick Van Orden told Kent in the Washington office. The former Chief of Naval Research hadn't conceded his official bearing when he retired. "We'll be better received if a man with more, ah, experience, takes the helm. Surely you can see that."

Kent couldn't, but compromised anyway. John Erthein (a former

175

Reagan fund-raiser) became president of the APA, and Kent, executive vice-president. Van Orden was designated vice-president of research. The APA paid Van Orden a full-time salary, though the man worked only three days a week. He also demanded a big staff to assist him. Overhead ran high, but so did Kent's hopes.

At an APA meeting in May, Regino Perez-Polo, Ph.D, a researcher and associate professor in the Department of Human Biological Chemistry and Genetics at the University of Texas Medical Center, spoke of optimism in research.

"The dictum taught in medical school is that there could be no regeneration of the central nervous system, so the paralysis was permanent," Perez-Polo said. "But within the past five years, a complete reversal of this thinking has occurred. It is clear the tools are available now."

Also discussed at this meeting were new findings concerning electrical treatments that provided tiny electric currents to injured bone and tissue. These treatments promoted regrowth. Kent smiled; he had undergone similar therapy in Russia.

Research moved along, and so did the organization.

"I still don't like it, Kent," Lynn said as they flew home that fall from yet another APA meeting. "I know lots of our sponsors recommended one organization, not three. And I understand the wisdom in that. But none of these folks can raise the kind of money you've been raising. *You* cultivated all the Texas sponsors. What exactly *is* the function of the rest of this group?"

Kent shook his head. "Not all the Texas sponsors," he countered.

Lynn stared evenly at him. "Most of them," she said. "And don't think the rest of this group doesn't resent that."

"Who?"

"Just about every one, especially those San Francisco socialites, the Aliotos. And Van Orden. And Camhi in New York and Marty Ergas in Florida. They want you to raise the money, and themselves get the credit and keep control."

"Now, Lynn," Kent began, touching her arm, "you're overreacting. They all *like* me, especially Joe Alioto. Well," Kent paused to chuckle, "everyone except maybe the Rear Admiral. The "Rear" part really fits that guy. But everybody's heart's in the right place — "

176

"They like you to your face, then take swipes at you behind your back."

"Look," he began, voice rising, "we all want the same thing. Marty himself is in a wheelchair from polio. With his own wealth and those he knows he can raise lots of money.

"David Camhi has already got the Stephen Camhi fund rolling, and that'll raise a hundred thousand or so a year. And I know Michelle Alioto is the debutante type, but they've already planned a big fund-raiser. Joe Alioto's the son of the former San Francisco mayor. Those are invaluable contacts.

"And," he continued quickly, "we've set a precedent for each board member to donate $25,000 a year. Think of all the money that'll put into research!"

"*If* that all happens," Lynn countered. "And in the meantime, they all look down on you because you're young and successful, then fight among themselves and rely on you, the kid, to soothe everybody's ego. This stinks, Kent."

"Well, we all know I don't have to worry about a big ego," Kent joked.

Lynn shot arrows into him from her blue-green eyes. For the first time, Kent felt the coldness — not originating with his wife, but as if transferred through her from the group. No.

"Look," he said, "I don't care who gets what credit."

"That's good — 'cause it won't be you," Lynn snapped.

"I just want to get money into research. That's all I care about. You know," he said and smiled, "it's hard to have an ego when somebody has to help you go to the bathroom."

Lynn stared at him a minute, shook her head, and smiled. Then she laughed and the tension dissolved. But the cold stone in the pit of Kent's stomach didn't dissipate with it. It'll be okay, he assured himself. He could hold these folks together.

That Kent remained in the spotlight did not help soothe those egos, however. The Dallas chapter of the National Society of Fund-Raising Executives named him Outstanding Professional Fund-Raiser of the Year for 1982. And in December Kent traveled to Alexandria, Virginia, for his first National Council on the Handicapped meeting. At twenty-eight years of age, Kent became the youngest appointee ever named to the fifteen-member council.

This National Council was the only federal agency mandated by Congress to address disability policy issues. It made policy for several other federal agencies and committees, such as the National Institute on Disability and Rehabilitation Research, the Rehabilitation Services Administration, and the President's Committee on Employment of Persons with Disabilities. Also the council was charged with reporting the state of disability in the nation to the president and Congress in an annual report. The Council had an annual budget of $198,000, which included one staff assistant and a small one-room office in the basement of the Department of Education.

Kent and Lynn awakened at five that morning in the Old Town Holiday Inn, where the first meeting was to take place. After completing the long ritual of bathing and dressing, Kent arrived in the conference room at 8:15 for the 8:30 kickoff.

Lynn wheeled him in saying, "No one here."

Kent looked nervously around. No coffee, juice, nor Danishes. Finally, others began to filter in and Lynn left.

The same stack of government papers and materials which Kent had been mailed prior to the meeting sat in front of each place. Amid the crackle of nervous laughter, an older, burly gentleman introduced himself.

"I am Joe Dusenberry," he began in a booming voice. "The chairman of the National Council on the Handicapped." Then to Kent's surprise, Dusenberry launched into a thirty-minute presentation on the life and times of Joe Dusenberry in vocational rehabilitation and national disability issues. *Good God.* The pretty blond woman next to him, Roxanne Vierra from Denver, groaned and rolled her eyes. They grinned to one another.

But though Dusenberry was not blessed with the gift of oration, as the Commissioner of the South Carolina Department of Vocational Rehabilitation he played a vital role in organizing vocational rehabilitation in America. Many honors graced his distinguished career. Kent and the disability community nationwide respected him.

Finally his half-hour introduction ended.

178

"Would each of you now give a brief description of your involvement with disability issues," he directed.

Sandra Parrino of New York was introduced, and she described her battles raising three sons with various disabilities. Kent admired her courage. The passion that flashed in her large eyes revealed an unrelenting commitment to their cause.

He was also pleased to meet Justin Dart, Jr., from Texas. Dart was known as the father of disability in Texas, and while they knew of each other, they'd never met.

All the members were equally impressive with career and personal achievements. Intimidated by their experience, Kent's frustration grew over his own lack of preparation as well. I *will* read every shred of paper and each government report before the next meeting, he vowed.

For two and a half more hours, Joe Dusenberry owned the microphone. He preached the gospel of disability according to Dusenberry, the gist of which was: "We must be careful not to draw attention to ourselves, because no one in the administration wants a National Council on the Handicapped. We can all be easily fired."

What? Then what the hell're we doing here? The White House doesn't want us? I don't believe that, Kent muttered under his breath.

The day progressed along these lines. Dusenberry proclaimed that their allocated funds allowed for little more than meeting the mandated four times per year. By the end of the day, drained and relatively discouraged, Kent thought of little but eating and enjoying a glass of wine.

Hilda, the staff assistant, convinced most of the group to trek down the street to an Italian restaurant. Kent and Lynn agreed, mostly because a bottle of cabernet had his name on it.

He thanked his lucky stars he went. For during dinner and nightcaps later, the ice cracked open. Everyone left with a feeling of common purpose, of how they could more effectively interact to survive as a Council. Kent slept, knowing even another Dusenberry sermon couldn't break the bond they established. This Council would be a catalyst for disability rights and policy, affecting changes for millions of Americans. Exactly *how* this would happen, he was not sure. But *that* it would, he felt certain. Yes, they'd make waves. Lots of them.

The year 1983 began with good press and terrible news. *People* magazine printed another feature on Kent, bringing the APA-much needed publicity. "Battling All the Way" again told his story, from the injury through the Russia trip to his first foundation.

"It was no coincidence that in the years after the birth of Waldrep's foundation," the article reported, "significant progress emerged in a number of areas of spinal cord research. With increased funding, much of which was raised from the private sector by Waldrep's group, researchers uncovered some startling new breakthroughs.

"A research group in Ohio showed that computer implants could be used to send impulses to a paraplegic's extremities. Other experimenters began developing drugs that could control hemorrhaging that occurs immediately after a spinal cord has been injured. Often it is this hemorrhaging that causes paralysis.

"Tests with enzymes began to open up another avenue of hope. Some doctors even began discussing the prospect that damaged spinal cord nerves could be made to regenerate — a notion that would have been scoffed at a few years earlier."

Touchdown, Kent thought, reading the story. Just what we need to raise some consciousness concerning paralysis. The public sector responded and fund-raising revenues shot skyward.

Then on Wednesday, January 26, 1983, Bear Bryant died. This cannot be, Kent thought. I cannot lose this man. The world cannot lose him. As he and Lynn traveled to Birmingham for the funeral, Kent felt the Bear's presence, much as he had those first few weeks in the hospital. Bad things happen on the 26th, he thought. Would that day always be his nemesis?

Coach Bryant had just retired, right after winning the Liberty Bowl. Kent talked with him earlier in the season, spoke with the man who'd always been there for him, through the toughest of times, the organizational fighting, the striving for dreams, the tragedies. The Bear was his friend. And now he was gone. What will I do when I need his advice, Kent wondered. Dear God, I didn't even get to say goodbye.

The weather in Birmingham was grey and cold and rainy. An incredible number of Bear's players came to the funeral — Joe Namath, Richard Todd, too many to count. They came to pay respects to the man who changed all their lives.

Sitting with the family, Kent wondered how many saw the other

180

side of the coach — the tenderness behind the gruff exterior. Had anyone but himself seen a tear in Bear Bryant's eye? Probably not, though everyone loved him.

The whole country mourned his passing, but nowhere as much as in Birmingham. People standing on the street were crying.

How lucky I was to have that man as a friend, Kent thought on the plane home. How special it was to see the other side — away from football. How I will miss him.

Back home, the publicity around the APA soared. Unfortunately, so did the board members' backstabbing. The ones with injured children wanted their offspring to be as successful as Kent. When that didn't occur, they became jealous and resentful. It's okay, he kept telling himself and Lynn — if this is what it takes to find a cure.

All the personalities involved wanted to be in the news, to raise the most money, to do what they wanted with it. This is *not* what we came together for, Kent thought, but there wasn't much he could do about it.

In San Francisco, Michelle Alioto organized a huge fund-raiser, grossing an enormous amount of money. Unfortunately, most of the gross went to pay expenses, with little net result. But her name and face graced newspapers and television so nothing Kent said could dampen her alleged success. Well, he figured, at least this keeps the paralysis question in the public eye.

Then 1983 brought another blow. Pat Holloway, who had given enormous amounts of money every year, first to the KWISCRF, then to the APA, lost his oil company in a legal fight with the widow of his partner. With that cash base gone, the sharks circled the water. John Erthein immediately resigned as president, and Kent took over. Turmoil intensified.

"What're you gonna do now, Kent," Van Orden stated, no question in his gruff voice.

Janet Reed, the office manager and executive vice-president of operations, sat next to Van Orden in her wheel chair. She often mimicked Van Orden's philosophies, and she now sat smirking.

Kent bit his tongue. He wanted to say, "Why don't you guys go out and raise some money, Mr. 'Rear' Admiral Van Ordinary?" Instead he answered, "We've got our fund-raising program in place now. We won't live or die based on one contributor."

But he worried. Holloway's money, while not the bulk of funds raised every year, *was* regular. Many board members panicked at the loss. Kent had taken great pains to spread the fund-raising out though, so losing Holloway really was more of a psychological mishap than a financial one.

Now, however, everyone wanted to keep money raised in their own part of the country. The organization, drawn together to pool resources for a paralysis cure, became more factionalized than before incorporation. Kent continued to soothe egos, trying to keep the personalities knitted together. But dealing with the likes of Michelle Alioto — who decided she needed her own office in San Francisco — took an enormous amount of time. Good grief. And every day, Van Ordinary repeated, "What're you gonna do now, Kent."

Van Orden also clashed regularly with the Science Advisory Committee. Always angry at someone, Van Orden kept the entire APA stirred up. Of course, he *knew* everything about everything, and much more than the scientists.

"This is totally against what we agreed," Kent finally said at a board meeting. "Our scientists manage the research program; our staff's not supposed to contradict everything they say."

On the surface, the board members all agreed with him. But behind his back, the slurs escalated. His frustration grew.

Still, research progressed — much of it funded by the APA. Much good was being done in spite of all the fighting.

In May of 1983, Dr. Jerrold Petrofsky of Wright State University testified before the House of Representatives, Subcommittee on Labor, Health, Human Services and Education. He recently made history with two young women, one a paraplegic, the other, quadriplegic. Both walked with the aid of a computerized, electrical stimulation and feedback system — for which the APA had provided the research grant.

Petrofsky stated, "One of the frustrating things we experience as research scientists working in this area is in knowing that you are so close to a cure. That a cure might be just years away, not decades, if only you had the funding to obtain the personnel and equipment to make it happen."

Get 'em, Petrofsky, Kent cheered.

Through the summer, the scientists researched, the APA raised

182

money to fund grants, and the board members feuded. During one awful meeting in Dallas, Lynn and Kent were called to the hospital where her dad was recovering from gall bladder surgery. Then unexpectedly, he died.

Through his grief, Kent was still forced to reckon with the APA's adversity. The Scientific Advisory Committee became more and more fed up — sick of having Van Orden contradict all their proposals.

And both Denise and Lynn began telling Kent to get out. "The patronization to your face and then doing the exact opposite is getting really old, Kent," Lynn said after yet another fight the couple had about Kent quitting. "I know it doesn't bother you so much, but it kills me to see you treated like this."

"I don't care who gets the credit," he replied, "whose name is at the top, or whose 'organization' it is."

"That's not the point," Lynn countered. "You're not getting the best people for the job, and that's *always* been your focus."

Kent sat silently, staring at his fingers.

"You deserve better," Lynn said. "We deserve better. A semblance of a normal life and family right here," she rubbed her fist across her heart.

"Life hasn't been exactly normal for me in a while," Kent said, spreading open his arms and gesturing at the chair. But he smiled.

Lynn added, "And children."

Kent looked into the beseeching eyes of his wife.

They *had* discussed children, but, Lord, not now. Not in the middle of all this crap.

"Lynn . . ."

"I know the time's not right, not this second. But it may take a long time to conceive anyway. Maybe by the time we do, you'll be outa this mess. I want a real life, Kent, with our own home. With children."

Kent sighed. She was right, of course. But he couldn't give up the fight for a cure. It was his life. He must find a way to do both.

In December of 1983, Kent and Lynn moved into their own home. For the first time, they made friends outside of the paralysis community and his parents' circle. They still saw Denise and Al all the time, but for once, Kent and Lynn lived a life on their own. Now, if he could just smooth over the APA woes, all would be perfect.

This of course did not happen and everyone continued to bicker.

In early 1984, the Waldreps' attorneys approached Kent with an out-of-court settlement on the artificial turf lawsuit.

"But the money's not the point," Kent argued. "I want a national debate on artificial turf."

"You have no choice," the faceless attorneys replied.

"Then why have we dragged this out for nine years?"

"Well, things have changed. New evidence has arisen that the field was not as damaged as we once thought. The case is not quite as strong as it originally was."

Kent rubbed his eyes. "I really don't care," he said. "I want to go to trial. My whole point has always been to outlaw artificial turf, and that's still my goal. New evidence or not."

"Mr. Waldrep," one attorney began, "you will lose. Not only is there the aforementioned evidence, but you, sir, have become entirely too successful to stand trial. Neither judge nor jury would feel the pity required to help your case."

"You've gotta be kidding," Kent blurted. "I'm too successful to convince a judge or jury that smashing onto a concrete football field is the only reason I'm in a wheelchair?"

Both attorneys stared, stone-faced.

"It has also been brought to our attention that you have been approached to file a lawsuit against TCU for their disclaiming of liability."

"And I refused. A long time ago. I don't want to sue my school or my team."

"That's very wise," the attorney continued. "You would not win that one either. Please consider this settlement. It is the best you can do."

For weeks, Kent struggled with the options. Denise, Al, and Lynn left the decision up to him. More than anything he wanted a national debate on artificial turf.

But what if the attorneys were right? Would losing set *back* that cause rather than help it?

He knew, too, that his mom and dad went deeply into debt to support and care for him since the accident. Not the sort of folks to declare bankruptcy, they would spend the rest of their lives paying back

184

that debt. The money would help them out and provide some financial security for Lynn and himself.

Reluctantly, Kent agreed to the settlement. But doing so left a hole in his belly nothing could fill.

Kent put some of the settlement to immediate use in the APA. The board had originally set a precedent of every member raising $25,000 per year as a contribution. Together, Joe and Michelle Alioto were behind big-time on their pledges. Some board members wanted the couple to resign.

One of the most frustrating situations Kent faced (as with any non-profit executive) is how to approach a board member about his or her lack of financial commitment to the cause. The first two responsibilities of board members are to "give" themselves and then "get" from others. There is no need to dwell on policy matters if the organization's resources cannot impact the mission.

So Kent anonymously lent the organization the $75,000, giving the Aliotos time to pay off their pledge. No one knew from where the money came. Kent left it that way.

Meanwhile, he continued fund-raising and all the things he had done since his accident. The 1982 Texas Tycoon Gala had been chaired by Norman and Nancy Brinker (he started Steak and Ale and Chili's; she founded the Susan B. Komen Foundation for Breast Cancer Research). Herman Lay, the founder of Frito-Lay, chaired the 1983 gala. Each year the funds raised increased. Also in 1983 the world premiere of Clint Eastwood's *Sudden Impact* in Houston raised $115,000 for the APA. And this year, Danny Faulkner was chairing the first No Gala Gala — an event to raise the funds without having an event.

Kent also often visited with spinal cord injured patients in the hospitals. One in particular tugged his heartstrings.

Joey Nichols was a good kid, and too young to be paralyzed. But driving home one night he had wrecked his car, and his spine. Something in Joey's eyes kept Kent coming back.

"You just gotta press on, man," Kent told the kid. "Pretty soon, those ounces you're lifting will turn into pounds. Things'll get better if you persevere. I promise."

Joey did get better. Nothing compared to the looks in the eyes of Joey and his dad, Joe, when Kent visited.

Not much was happening on the National Council on the Handicapped, until finally that year Dusenberry's perception of the White House "wanting them to disappear" was proven wrong: Reagan replaced him. The vice-chair, Sandi Parrino, became the chair. And the first order of business was to change that damn name. They became the National Council on Disability. And now they changed its course.

In September of 1984, the movie *The Bear* premiered in Birmingham, and Kent once again traveled to the city. The marketing company for the movie had offices in the same building as the APA in Dallas. The company aligned the project with the APA. It was so special, Kent thought, to again travel to Alabama, and once more honor Bear Bryant.

The state police again escorted the Waldreps to the hotel. They received the same treatment as when they had returned for that first game after the accident. TCU never honored him at a game, but ten years later, Alabamans hadn't forgotten. How he loved these folks.

A thousand people attended the dinner and premier — shown at four theaters. Just before the movie started, President Reagan called Kent to congratulate him on the project. *Good Morning America* covered the premier. Though the movie was never endorsed by the Bryant family, "Alabama" attended the event. Seventy-five thousand more needed dollars were raised. How odd, Kent thought, that in the midst of turmoil such good things happen.

More excellent news came from the research community as well. Though Wise Young and the National Acute Spinal Cord Injury Study was not complete, Young continued researching both early drug treatments and the study of the basis of recovery after cord injury. The results, Young said, revolutionized his thinking about spinal cord injury. The mammalian central nervous system contained hundreds of thousands of axons. But with only 1 to 2 percent of those axons intact, animals could walk again.

"In my lifetime," Young stated, "before the end of the century, techniques will be available to regenerate 1 to 2 percent of the axons in the spinal cord. The central nervous system is capable of regeneration. I am absolutely convinced we will be able to improve the function of axons."

Another researcher, Albert Aguayo in Montreal at McGill University and Montreal General Hospital, proved through his experiments what had long been suspected: properly nurtured central axons *can* regenerate; the permissive environment of the peripheral system provides the stimulus for regeneration.

Though no one was saying outright what this meant, everyone knew — with guarded optimism — what it could mean.

All this made the struggles within the APA all the more frustrating, and none more so than Van Orden's continued friction with their Science Advisory Committee.

As Kent focused on raising money for a cure (the No Gala Gala raised another $120,000) the APA problems started to boil. And as 1985 began, the in-fighting threatened to rip apart the organization.

In January, Kent and Lynn traveled to Tulsa, where Kent accepted an honor from the United States Jaycees. They named him one of the Ten Outstanding Young Men of America.

One week later, Kent flew to New York City for a meeting with the APA's Science Advisory Committee — all of whom were going to resign because of Van Orden. Kent promised to end the fighting once and for all.

He was also scheduled to journey to Japan for an important paralysis conference, hosted by Shell Oil Company. Board members Louie and Dell Rice set up his trip. Kent had to go.

Before leaving for Japan, he fired Van Orden and left Rita Cole, the vice-president of finance in the Dallas office, in charge.

The Japan meeting proved very successful. But when Kent returned, he found Van Orden still there. The military strategist had lobbied the board — all of whom professed to support Kent on the firing decision. Now the board pointed fingers at Kent. They were angry he left for Japan, no matter how important that meeting.

Van Orden said Kent could not fire him and that Kent should be ousted. A board meeting was called for early March in San Diego.

In the meantime, Hank Stifel, a wealthy New Jersey businessman and new board member, was playing games. To Kent's face, Stifel continually praised his efforts and pledged support. But behind the scenes the businessman hedged bets. His influence upon the other APA members escalated.

At the board meeting, controversy peaked again over money owed by members. And, it was commonly held that Marty Ergas had covered for the Aliotos.

Finally, Kent spoke. "I lent the money to the organization," he said.

For a second, dead silence filled the room. Then the bickering boiled over.

Lynn accompanied Kent to San Diego for this meeting, but at the end of the day, she could not be found. Many hours later, she returned to the hotel.

"This is *it*, Kent. Let's go."

"I can't just go. The meeting's not over yet."

"I mean resign. Leave."

Kent's blood ran cold. Was this the right move? He trusted Lynn's judgment, but he couldn't just quit, could he? Not without one more fight.

At the end of the meeting, Kent asked for a vote of confidence. He received it, but the vote was not unanimous. Four of the twenty board members voted nay: Hank Stifel (who had proclaimed to support Kent all along), the Aliotos, and Dell Rice.

With a heavy heart, Kent returned to Dallas with Lynn. His wife hardly spoke to him. In his gut, Kent knew she'd been right.

Soon after the meeting, board members began contacting him.

"We want to work with you," they all said, "and get Van Orden out. Let's move the main office from Dallas to New York, cut the staff in Dallas, and you can move to New York as well."

This was every bit about control. Kent saw the road ahead, with no way to alter the course. The momentum had shifted too far to the other side.

Another board meeting was called for April in Washington, D.C. Van Orden agreed to resign, as did Janet Reed. Kent agreed to cut the staff in Dallas. But no, he would not move to New York. And actually, the move was not to New York at all, but to New Jersey — and into Hank Stifel's offices.

The end neared.

In May, Kent received a call from some fund-raisers in California. The APA initiated a golf tournament in L.A., headed by a woman with an injured son and a man with one as well. They controlled the money from the event and wanted to spend it on a local doctor, one who was not approved by the APA's Science Advisory Committee.

It appeared they were going to do just that. Kent immediately wire-transferred the money to pay research contracts already due.

All hell broke loose. Camhi accused Kent of using the money to pay himself back on the $75,000 loan.

An emergency board meeting was called in Dallas in late May. Following the usual fighting, Kent began to speak. He voiced all his concerns.

"There has been so much compromise here, and what's resulted has been totally against what we'd originally agreed upon. We spend so much money on research staff and then let that staff argue with our scientists. We fight each other constantly. Have we completely lost sight of our mission?

"When the Kent Waldrep International Spinal Cord Research Foundation negotiated a merger with the Paralysis Cure Foundation, it was to pool our resources in order to effectively help research a cure for paralysis. We've gotten away from our mission, and the course we're on is *not* why I got involved. If, however, this is what you all want, I don't want any part of it. We are doing a huge disservice to the injured community. Now, you decide." And with that, Kent left the room.

For four hours, Kent, Denise, Al, and a group of close friends hung around the hotel lobby. Kent stared at the walls. But he knew in his heart he'd done all he could. And also in his heart, he knew what the outcome would be.

Denise Waldrep watched her son fidget in his wheel chair. The hours since he'd spoken to the APA board of directors dragged on. Standing up to these people was the right thing to do. She told Kent that and how proud she was of him. It didn't ease the pain much.

She hadn't truly known of the troubles with the APA, not until that spring and, really, until that very day. She saw now that Kent wanted to shield her from it.

Since Kent and Lynn no longer lived with Al and her, the day-to-day running of the organization was now foreign to Denise. She had no earthly idea that things were at this point — not until Kent emerged from the conference room, his shattered gaze upon her. How difficult it now was to stay silent.

Her son started the Kent Waldrep International Spinal Cord Research Foundation after returning from Russia to such an enthusiastic response. This response came both from the general public, and from scientists concerned about the lack of research funds available. The Waldreps had been so elated to hear that people actually wanted to do something about the problem.

For so long they were told that nothing could be done. When scientists wanted to actively research, the Waldreps' minds completely opened to those needs. They thought of nothing but beginning as quickly as possible. Kent soared to heaven.

He worked like there was no tomorrow. Her boy wrote the book on persistence. Denise smiled, remembering Kent inducing a pleurisy attack while playing golf on a family vacation when he was in the eighth grade. He had played all day from sunrise until darkness caught him — not listening to reason, but giving his all to the golf course. The sixth day of this golf marathon found him with aches and a high fever.

A trip to the emergency room brought the pleurisy diagnosis. Kent never learned when to quit anything.

Denise never quite forgave her son for not accepting a golf scholarship to college. "I'll take it back up after football — if I'm not drafted," he always said. To this day, Kent still felt his golf swing. While watching golf on television, he imagined gripping the club, addressing the ball, taking the backswing then the club into impact and follow-through. He possessed all the natural talent to be a golf great and all the tenacity to make it happen.

Kent strove to win every game he played — from golf to monopoly. But Denise knew he would not win this one.

From the beginning, she had voiced concerns about this merger. Kent had worked *so hard,* with only one purpose in mind. But he assured both parents that the ideas would remain the same, that most of the people involved had children who were spinal cord injured, and they wanted the same things from the foundation as the KWISCRF did. By working together they could accomplish this much faster. It all made sense at the time.

These thoughts drifted through Denise's mind as she watched the fallen face of her son. She knew this board knew exactly what they were going to do when the meeting was called. Had people ever been so underhanded? These men and women who only a few years earlier asked for his help and leadership were now destroying the very thing Kent built and gave his life to.

He was no match for them. He didn't have practice in such dealings. His only goal was to find a cure for paralysis the fastest way possible. How could human beings be so cruel? How could they completely steal something so close to a man's heart and soul? So many years had passed since her son had been this hurt. Denise vowed that no one would ever do anything like this to him again, not while she and Al were around.

One of the board members emerged from the room. Matter-of-factly, he informed Kent of the new structure, with the national office to be in New Jersey. They wanted Kent to stay on for P.R. and fund-raising. All the original board members of the KWISCRF resigned.

Denise watched as without one moment's hesitation, Kent Waldrep resigned from the organization he had created. A huge weight seemed lifted from his shoulders and though his eyes filled with tears, Kent smiled up at her. He might be a long time recovering from this one, but as with all the other blows he'd been dealt, Denise knew her son would, indeed, overcome.

✧ CHAPTER THIRTEEN ✧

DISABILITY IN AMERICA: PATHOLOGY OR CULTURE?

After the resignations, many of Kent's original board members, some friends, Denise, Al, and Kent went to dinner.

Lynn stayed home — both devastated and relieved. Life-long family friends from El Paso, Walter and Tricia Stowe, and from Grand Prairie, Sam and Betty Pettigrew, stayed with the Waldreps all day, offering support and love. Sitting at dinner, Kent felt the caring of all these folks surround him. He would be grateful for life.

"You know I'm behind you 100 percent," board member Linda Allison said. "We all are."

Kent answered quietly, "I know."

And he did know. Lamar Hunt said the same thing before they left the hotel. Pat Holloway had been neck-deep in lawyers down in Austin, but flew in anyway to lend support. Holloway also gave the board a good Texas tongue-lashing.

Real estate tycoon Danny Faulkner and his running buddies carried most of the conversation that night. Faulkner had given generously to the foundation and suggested the dinner after the long day. Though Kent was a bit wary since Faulkner had been the subject of a series of *Dallas Morning News* allegations regarding shady real estate dealings, he wanted to believe Faulkner's promises that it was all untrue and that he sincerely wanted to help.

Kent hardly heard their dialogue. He, Linda Allison, Denise, and Al were all unusually quiet. He did hear retired pro-bowl Dallas Cowboy Cliff Harris say, "We can't let this go. Let's take names and kick ass," reminding everyone why he had gained the nickname, "Captain Crash."

192

Many of the others were equally defiant. The emotions around Kent were stretched to the breaking point, and voices rose. But the day's events kept replaying in his mind.

Had the board members acted from conscience? Did they truly believe this was the best thing? Were they swayed by the political maneuverings of the few? No matter, I know I did the right thing. But please, God, show me the way from here.

At 3:00 a.m., as Lynn and Kent lay awake in the darkness of their bedroom, Kent said, "I'm gonna start over. I'm gonna create a new foundation."

Though Lynn lay silent, Kent knew this was the right thing to do. And in that darkness, peace enveloped him.

At first, his folks and Lynn opposed the idea. He understood their fears. So much happened since the start of the KWISCRF. Lynn wanted him to spend time on more productive pursuits. Denise worried her son might again get badly bruised.

"I can't sit by and watch anyone do this sort of thing to you again," Denise told him. "Never again. No one will *ever* hurt my son like that another time."

Kent rubbed his chin with the back of his hand and then calmly said, "Mom, this is what I'm supposed to do. I *have* to start all over again."

Denise eyed him. Her stare always bored clean through to his heart, but he didn't look away.

"Well," Denise said slowly, "I don't want you to roll over and play dead, either. If you're *sure*," she said softly, paused, and then continued, "if you know for certain this is what you want, then go for it. If you can dive back into this sea, then your dad and I can also."

For two weeks after Kent's resignation, the APA board tried to talk him into staying on. He refused. The organization he founded then cut him loose without even the courtesy of severance pay.

By July 1, 1985, Kent reincorporated into a new organization. The Kent Waldrep National Paralysis Foundation was formed. Nothing ever felt more right.

Danny Faulkner gave them office space for the first six months, along with a generous cash donation. All the board members reassured Kent that they believed in him and his direction. As Cliff Harris said, "I'm relieved you resigned, Kent, because I know what you're trying to do — form a big, national organization to crystallize awareness and research. We're with you."

Fund-raising began anew, in earnest. NFL Charities gave the NPF its first grant. People from Kent's past materialized to help, including Joey Nichols's father, Joe. Nichols told the press, "To a guy whose whole life had been knocked down, to see someone like Kent looking so good and know that you could get better, was so encouraging. . . . I can't explain it." The foundation was off and running.

And so were Kent and Lynn's plans of beginning a family. They both had already undergone fertility tests, and *both* were found capable of having a child. Yes, the doctors had falsely predicted Kent's capabilities once again. Actual conception would require some tricky maneuvering, but, Kent reasoned, if God meant it to be, then it would.

He endured the painful collection process. The doctors warned that this might send his blood pressure soaring, which it did, and his physiological reaction to that resulted in a migraine headache of terrible and fluctuating proportions. He remained in bed for a week.

Lynn underwent artificial insemination. For three weeks, they waited anxiously to see if the process had worked, if they had conceived. They had not.

"It's okay," Kent assured her. "We still have lots of time."

His wife looked at him, her clear eyes liquid and soft.

Lynn's desire for children had grown like a California wildfire over the past few years, and she became increasingly despondent. That it was in God's hands would not comfort her at this instant, Kent knew, so he kept that quiet. In his heart, though, he wasn't worried.

Meanwhile, Wise Young completed the National Acute Spinal Cord Injury Study. The results were promising, but inconclusive. They received a grant that enabled the study to continue as Part II.

When not fund-raising, running the new foundation, or trying to conceive a child, Kent worked on the National Council on Disability. They focused on six main areas: (1) coordination of special education and vocational rehabilitation; (2) improved interface of vocational rehabilitation and private enterprise; (3) establishment of model centers for employment of the disabled; (4) disability prevention through improved health education and secondary prevention initiatives; (5) elevating the effectiveness of federal disability programs; (6) strengthening the Social Security system by eliminating disincentives to employment.

Constantly amazed by the bureaucratic monster that ran Washington, Kent and the council kept fighting the old guard. Kent grouped the good-old-boy networks into four categories:

1. the unenlightened and unknowledgeable legislators and staffers writing laws and regulations;

2. the paid disability lobbyists who make their living off disability;

3. federal appointees to disability agencies and councils; and

4. the disability advocates outside government.

Kent found that the old guard with tired ideas tried to strangle change. He told Lynn, "A bureaucracy allows for old ideas to live on long after detectable brain activity has stopped."

But the council just kept firmly moving toward its goals. And as 1985 rumbled to a close and the council met at the same Old Town Holiday Inn, each member expressed a growing optimism, a feeling of change. A new era, under the direction of Sandra Parrino, with Kent elected as vice-chairman, had begun. Sandy was, indeed, a ball of fire and Kent admired her greatly. Old ideas were consistently challenged and the status quo not tolerated. Now was the time not only for polls and reports and public forums, but for disability legislation as well.

In an attempt to understand the "politics" of working inside the beltway that surrounds the District of Columbia and to keep his perspective clear, Kent authored his own "Beltway Rules":

1. Power is everything.

2. Perception is more powerful than fact.

3. Yes, means, "I'm keeping my options open."

4. No, means, "I'm keeping my options open."

5. Knife-throwing is a sport exceeded only by fence-sitting.

6. The system wins 95 percent of the time.

7. Being a fiscal conservative still allows you to build up huge campaign debts.

8. The pope could be corrupted if he stayed in Washington long enough.

9. Senility is the common thread linking the Republicans and Democrats.

10. "Twenty something" staffers control most legislation.

11. Productivity is a Japanese word.

12. The boss is underpaid and the employee is overpaid (when compared to the private sector).

13. The words you speak today may be your dinner tomorrow.

14. If all else fails, refer to rule number one.

Despite these rules and facing the old-guard resistance, the National Council on Disability *was* getting somewhere. In 1986 the Americans with Disabilities Act was conceived and proposed. It would be a while in the drafting process but, when complete, would assure a new direction for disability policy in America — one that offered equal opportunity, encouraged full participation, and moved away from an entitlement mentality. Kent recommended the title for the law, and the rest of the council agreed upon it.

Throughout 1986, the National Paralysis Foundation grew. Locally, the foundation worked with the University of Texas at Arlington Center for Advanced Rehabilitation Engineering, the Human Performance Institute, at St. Paul Medical Center, the Dallas Rehabilitation Institute and the Baylor College of Medicine in Houston.

Also in 1986 Danny Faulkner was indicted in the I-30 real estate scandal, and the board asked him to resign. Faulkner had all along insisted on his innocence to Kent and everyone. Kent liked Danny. And the man had donated over $200,000. But his troubles had started having a negative impact on the foundation. Likeable as he was, Danny could no longer be involved.

In Austin, the Jaycees decided to allot the funds raised from their golf tournament to the National Paralysis Foundation. The tournament's chairman, Doug English, was an old acquaintance of Kent's from college football days. Doug played for the University of Texas

196

at the same time Kent did for TCU. An All-American at the University of Texas, Doug went on to become an All-Pro defensive tackle for the Detroit Lions. His career had ended with a ruptured disk, causing slight paralysis in his hands and left leg. Luckily, this paralysis had been temporary.

Kent felt an instant, almost mystic connection with Doug, and the feeling was reciprocated. They planned to play golf together, when Kent became able.

Odd, Kent thought, how football remained in his life through former players. Mike Renfro, a TCU teammate, had gone on to play wide receiver for the Houston Oilers and then the Dallas Cowboys. He now supported the foundation's fund-raising efforts, especially through golf tournaments. Renfro had brought in the play that fateful day in Alabama — the last down of football Kent ever played.

And of course, Roger Staubach always helped, and Cliff Harris and a host of others. They often joked that Cliff only showed up on the golf course to get pointers from Kent on his game. This tended to shock folks — when Kent, with uncanny accuracy, coached Cliff on his swing. Nothing shocked people as much, though, as Kent and Doug English's standing golf date.

NFL Charities again donated $20,000, and the by-invitation Texas Tycoon Gala held at Southfork ranch in November netted over $100,000 — a far, far cry from his first fund-raising fiasco. Kent set a goal of $2 million per year to sustain research.

In 1987 President Reagan reappointed Kent to a third term on the council, and the group began the actual writing of the Americans with Disabilities Act. Though progress seemed exasperatingly slow, Kent knew it actually went quick, for Washington time.

Throughout this period, he and Lynn still worked on a family. She underwent artificial insemination many times, to no avail. Reading voraciously on the topic, Lynn learned that the process could be done at home. So, in March of 1987, they tried it.

"How was I?" Kent quipped.

"Great," Lynn shot back, "what a lover!"

As the weeks passed, they gave one another conspiratorial looks and giggles. The night before doing the pregnancy test, Lynn said, "This is like a joint science project."

"Are you gonna break the news to me over candlelight and roses?" Kent asked and she laughed. Lynn had related her fantasy of telling him in romantic fashion. But they got so scientific about the whole thing, most of the suspense, as well as the romance, flew south for the season.

The next morning, Lynn did the test. It was positive.

From originally being told he would never have children, to struggling for years to conceive, researching, testing, striving — all the things that able and disabled folks try and try — the news sounded so simple, so clear, so easy. They would have a baby. Around Christmas.

Mentally down on his knees, Kent thanked God — and asked Him to quell this fear in his heart. A child. He was going to be a father. Could he do it? How much of an extra load would this be on Lynn? Could she do it? Would his weakened sperm somehow increase the chances for birth defects? Of course they had spoken of and planned for these things ad nauseam. But it's different when the reality actually occurs. What if he had a son who wanted to play football?

Denise and Al were beside themselves with joy. The family made an executive decision: Kent, Lynn, her mother, Jane, Denise, Al, and Kent's grandmother would all build a home together. "Southfork West," they called it. This child would be well cared for. And well loved.

Also in 1987 Texas Governor Bill Clements appointed Kent chairman of the Governor's Committee for Disabled Persons.

Kent smiled a lot that fall. How blessed they were! Lynn's pregnancy progressed well. The new foundation was thriving. Their money situation was holding, though the APA still hadn't completely paid back the money he lent them. Next year, they said.

The only chink in the picture came from TCU. Back in 1975 Jim Garner (then TCU's Sports Information Director), reserved a special seating area for Kent in the press box at Amon Carter Stadium. In 1987 this seating was replaced by a Coke machine.

Christmas drew near, its festivities brighter than usual this year. On Christmas Eve, Lynn went into labor. Alvis Kent Waldrep III was born soon after. They called him Trey. Announcing to the waiting room that they had a robust, beautiful son, Kent cried like a baby.

He held the healthy, six-and-a-half-pound, cloth-covered boy in his

198

arms. Everything else faded from view as he marveled at the tiny fingertips grasping his own. The turmoil of the last thirteen years was as if from another lifetime. In this hospital room there were no politics, no backstabbing, not even a quest. He felt no wheelchair. There was only his wife and his newborn son.

Complete love enveloped him — for Lynn, for being a father. This healthy, wondrous baby was God's gift to Lynn as much as me, he thought, for all her sacrifice. I need to plan for college now. And for when he asks me to play football.

When two days later he brought Lynn and Trey home to Plano, the press followed their departure.

"Having Trey resulted in a rebirth for both Lynn and me," Kent said. "I've never experienced anything so intense. And to be able to raise my son in an environment filled with so much love is the ultimate."

Yes, Kent thought as 1988 rolled in, I have most surely been blessed.

The Council got a shot in the arm from the results of two surveys, taken in 1986 and 1987. The National Council on Disability, in conjunction with the International Center for the Disabled, commissioned the surveys by Louis Harris and Associates entitled, *Bringing Disabled Persons into the Mainstream,* and *Employing Disabled Americans.* Together, they presented a composite picture of the many barriers faced by persons with disabilities in this country:

- Disabled Americans are much poorer than are nondisabled Americans. Half of all the disabled persons surveyed reported household incomes of $15,000 or less.

- Not working is perhaps the truest definition of what it means to be disabled: two-thirds of all disabled Americans between the ages of sixteen and sixty-four are not working. Only one in four work full-time and another 10 percent work part-time.

- A large majority of those not working say they want to work. Sixty-six percent of working-age disabled persons, who are not working, say they want to.

- Persons with disabilities, as a group, have far less education than their nondisabled peers. Forty percent of all disabled persons do not finish high school — nearly three times that of nondisabled Americans.

• Overwhelming majorities of managers gave disabled employees a good or excellent rating on their overall job performance. Only twenty managers said that their disabled employees job performance was fair, and virtually no one said they do poor work.

• Large majorities of managers said that making accommodations for disabled employees is not expensive. The cost of accommodations rarely drives the cost of employment above the average costs for all employees.

How different, Kent thought, the entire issue of disability is today than it was at the time of my injury. The attitude of "no hope ever" had disappeared, being replaced by the real possibility of a cure for paralysis.

The attitude fostered by rehab centers was now one of hope. T.I.I.R, where he had stayed for three months of acute rehab, was now one of the finest, most modern facilities for instituting such hope.

In April of 1988, the National Council on Disability unveiled the Americans with Disabilities Act at a Capitol Hill press conference. Few media folks and little fanfare accompanied the unveiling of a bill with forty-three million Americans with disabilities behind it.

The proposed law sought to prohibit discrimination on the basis of handicap in areas such as employment, housing, public accommodations, travel, communications, and activities of state and local government.

It specifically defined discrimination but also specified those actions that do not constitute discrimination. No existing disability-related laws — federal or state, and the state laws were stronger — would be overturned.

And, for the first time, enforcement procedures included administrative remedies, private right of action in federal court, monetary damages, injunctive relief, attorney's fees, and cutoffs of federal funds.

In January of 1990, Kent saw his dream of a major paralysis research center in Texas come true. In the spring of 1989, Kent had proposed to the University of Texas Southwestern Medical School in Dallas his vision of a major thrust into basic nerve regeneration research. Dr. Kern

Wildenthal, the president of the medical center complex, and Kent struck up an immediate friendship. They planned, and on January 13, 1990, raised the initial $1,000,000 to launch the program at a black-tie dinner, hosted by the Fina Corporation. With a goal of a $10,000,000 endowment, the new center would recruit a world-class faculty.

Also in April of that year, the Kent Waldrep National Paralysis Foundation sponsored an International Symposium on Neurotrauma at the University of North Texas in Denton. There, Dr. Jerald Bernstein, Chief of the Laboratory of Central Nervous System Injury for the V.A. Medical Center in Washington, D.C., reported nerve grafting to be one of the best hopes for correcting paralysis caused by spinal injuries. It replaced damaged nerve tissue with new tissue.

"Nerve grafting will be the wave of the future," Bernstein said.

The future of spinal cord injury research *was* here. It survived due to the scientists who refused concession in the face of diminishing federal grants and constant struggles to raise money from the public sector. Kent vowed those scientists would keep getting grants.

They were just too close now. Many researchers postulated that a cure waited around the next bend — to be found by the turn of the century. As the signing of the ADA grew closer, Kent spoke more and more about the need for attention to both disability issues and dollars for research.

"An estimated 43 million Americans are part of the largest minority class in our society — those with disabilities," he said, speaking to the sold-out state convention of the Texas Jaycees. "It is a microcosm of our nation. Disability touches our children and our grandparents; every color and religion; the poor and the rich; the uneducated and the Harvard graduate; the disadvantaged and those born with opportunity. It is a minority class that you can be born into or have the chance to join at any second of your life.

"Disability very often is the only common denominator that links the many and varied cultures of our nation. It transcends language and cultural differences. And disability can provide the catalyst for creating coalitions to fight for changes.

"Disability in America is not an issue that will fade away. In fact, disability will parallel the advances in medical technology. The number of severely disabled and elderly disabled will drastically increase as medicine strains to prolong death and encourage life, when neither circumstance may offer a quality of life worth living. That is unless our nation's disability policy is overhauled and retargeted."

More and more people were listening.

In 1990 the National Acute Spinal Cord Injury Study II was completed. The results of Wise Young et al. were astounding. They showed that patients treated with huge doses of the steroid drug methylprednisolone within eight hours after spinal cord injury recovered drastically more function than those not receiving it. Methylprednisolone reduced swelling in injured tissue, preventing secondary cell degeneration — the cause of much paralysis.

Kent smiled. The Russians used a precursor to methylprednisolone decades before. Kent received it at the Polenov Institute in Leningrad.

Through his mind drifted the American medical dogma of that time: *Any paralysis present three to six months after spinal cord injury is permanent.* Today few professionals held to that line of thought. Today the hope once labeled false stood on the verge of reality.

On July 26, 1990, President George Bush signed the Americans with Disabilities Act into law. Kent attended the White House ceremony. Watching the political maneuverings, he thought of how far the council and disability as a whole had come. And he thought of the changes in his own life these past sixteen years.

Since 1986 the council had authored the first status reports on disability — including *Toward Independence,* which stressed the need for the ADA — had commissioned the first Louis Harris polls on disability, had conceived and drafted this law, which the president now signed, had initiated the first national disability prevention program at the Centers for Disease Control, had held public forums on disability in all fifty states, and had initiated national studies into special education, technology, health insurance, and personal assistance care.

They not only authored the reports, but successfully fought with the White House and Congress for changes. They were not, Kent thought as President Bush's pen graced the paper, by any means finished.

We will write a national disability employment policy because the ADA itself will not provide jobs for many who have never worked. We will also ensure that legislation on disability prevention and personal assistance care become law.

But sitting there Kent knew there was much more than a legal fight ahead. Most of all, we must put to rest the idea of a disability culture. Today's disability leadership segregates the community by promoting deaf-only issues or blind-only issues or wheelchair-only issues. It ignores the parents' right to advocate and lead. And it condones and perpetuates age-old federal programs and appointed committees that fulfill no purpose and offer no solutions.

Tears welled in Kent's eyes as President Bush finished. What a special opportunity it has been for me to serve, he thought, and my voice be heard. Helping to conceive and draft the ADA, being the person who recommended its very name, I have finally made a difference. But my main battle is still to be fought. It is, as it has always been, one of changing attitudes. It is a battle I will never quit fighting.

This ceremony occurred at a time when the White House threatened to veto a rights measure that would overthrow several recent Supreme Court decisions that civil rights groups said made it harder for minorities to seek legal remedies for alleged discrimination.

What is needed in this country is a change of heart, he thought. Through his own disability, Kent felt prejudice and discrimination, though not nearly to the extent a nonwhite must endure. It is the hearts of those born white, and the heart of our nation as a whole, that must one day erase any barriers that separate our people because of skin color or disability. Please God, let my now toddling son, Trey, grow up in a world where people are judged by their God-given talents and not their physical hardware. A world where special education will become truly integrated and children with disabilities will learn in classrooms together with their nondisabled classmates. Those will be the children to mature into adulthood with a greater appreciation for every person's special talent and contribution to society.

Thinking of Trey, Kent grew homesick. As the ceremony ended and the politicians and paid lobbyists patted one another on the backs, Kent smiled and nodded, wanting only to feel the warmth of his home, his wife's arms around him, his son in his lap.

One day, he thought, when wheelchairs exist only in museums, I will run beside Trey and my second child, soon to be born, and teach them both to play golf. Along with millions like me, I will walk from my chair to engage in all the physical activities that others take for granted.

Kent paused, looking into the beautiful blue of God's sky and knowing in his heart this would come to pass. For in addition to his still recurrent dreams of running and playing golf, a new one filtered up. In it he held Lynn lightly yet firmly in his arms. And they were dancing.

THE OTHER SIDE OF THE RAINBOW

I had a dream last night,
 We were dancing together as you looked up in my eyes,
We whirled and twirled,
 And held each other so tight —
Yes, I had a dream last night.

 CHORUS:

  And I had a dream of the day,
   We all run in a park,
  When it matters not
   If your skin's light or dark,
  We all look at each other
   Casting no stones,
  Walk hand in hand and all get along.

When I awoke, I prayed,
 My dream is how it will be,
Knowing inside there's no impossible dreams,
 Except the ones you leave in your sleep —
Yes, I had a dream last night.

 CHORUS

When a man is a man,
 No matter how he stands,
But rather what he stands for,
 And you always can reach
The other side of the Rainbow,
 Regardless of touchdowns and yards.

Yes, I had a dream last night
A dream I'll dream every day of
 My life.

✦ EPILOGUE ✦

THE DIFFICULT WE DO TODAY: THE IMPOSSIBLE TAKES A LITTLE LONGER

Well, here we are. I started writing this book on airplanes, in hotel lobbies, between meetings, and on weekends. After three years I had finished parts of six chapters. It was time to get a professional involved.

I have a lot of friends in sports journalism, and it would have been easy to have given any one of them this book to write. But I wanted more than a sports perspective and more than just my story.

I hope now that you feel you know what the Waldrep family and friends faced after Kent Waldrep broke his neck. That's why Susan Malone became my partner on this book.

Susan came into my life just when she was supposed to — the good Lord's subtle way of reminding me that there is a bigger "plan." The Lord's emissary was my friend Larry Goldman, who worked with Susan in a writer's group in Euless, Texas.

I liked her from the start. It was important to me to have my family's perspective told and a message left with you, the reader, that this is not another ex-jock reliving his glory days in sports.

I mean, how terrific can it be to have your athletic career remembered for a broken neck? Not the fact that in one game I carried the football five times for five touchdowns and over 250 yards. Or that over my athletic career I rushed for touchdowns, passed for touchdowns, intercepted passes, recovered fumbles, kicked field goals, punted, kicked off, caught touchdown passes, pitched a no-hitter, hit homeruns, never struck out, won one-hundred-, two-hundred-, and four-hundred-meter races, won the broad jump, anchored winning sprint and mile relay

205

teams, won basketball games with last-second shots, won swimming meets, won golf tournaments.

Sports provided me the opportunity to learn what it takes to win. But to win you have to hate losing. You can never be satisfied with losing in sports. No one remembers who finished Number 2 in anything.

Life is different. The lessons of life often don't result in any clear winner or loser. And many times the competition in life is simply for survival, not some Super Bowl trophy.

I find it a paradox that in football, fourth and long would offer but one option: to punt.

In life, we all face fourth-and-long challenges, and I profess we again have but one option: to go for it!

We must all realize that each of us is unique with a special purpose and opportunity to leave our footprint on the map of humankind.

At this point in my life I am quite satisfied and proud of the opportunities I have had to make a difference.

Helping give birth to the paralysis research movement and funding the research that is now allowing people, like New York Jet Dennis Byrd and American League umpire Steve Palermo, to walk following injury is very rewarding for the heart and soul.

Being one of a handful who decided equal opportunity for those with disabilities meant writing a new law, which I named the Americans with Disabilities Act, is an experience that I will proudly relate to my grandchildren. Every time I hear the acronym ADA, I get chills knowing I named it.

But being a father, a husband, a son, a brother, and a friend is what motivates me for the future. I know I can help win the war against paralysis. Anybody who truly knows me realizes that somehow, some-way, I will make a cure a reality. And soon enough for me to still make a mint playing professional golf!

What I want to happen is for Kent Waldrep to be a better husband to Lynn, a better father to Trey and Charley, a better son to Mom and Dad, a better brother to Carole and Terry Lynn, and a better friend to those who love me and my family. That is my true challenge for the future.

God has brightly lit my life's career path, and I am excited about what I know will happen. It is a true blessing to be involved and to encourage others to give their best. But for me, life's greatest gift is the relationships we share with each other.

At the top is being a father. It is no doubt life's greatest love affair. Trey and Charley can extract from me the most intense feelings of love and frustration — and both in the span of seconds! I can only anticipate the joy and heartache that await Lynn and me as they grow to become young men.

I would sacrifice my life for theirs in a heartbeat. And isn't that one of life's greatest lessons and demands? We must all learn to sacrifice to truly appreciate — helping a cause, helping each other, or simply realizing that we all have a role. But it happens one person at a time. You make a decision to be your best, to help others not so blessed, and you find that the love within us lives in those we touch long after our bones and flesh are dust.

My will to walk is not motivated by a selfish desire to escape some horrible prison on wheels. My life is blessed — wheels or no wheels. My will is driven by a burning desire to forever bury medicine's antiquated history of imposing limits on people, because of its own failures or lack of vision. Nothing in medicine has ever been possible until it happened.

Every human being deserves hope. I believe we can treat disease and injury without stripping away hope.

In my lifetime I will work toward making the fourth-and-long decision to be one based on hope, on the will to always go for it, and on the faith to know we can.